Breed Lover's Guide™

PEMBROKE WELSH CORGI

A Practical Guide for the Pembroke Welsh Corgi Lover

Susan M. Ewing

Pembroke Welsh Corgi

Project Team
Editor: Stephanie Fornino
Indexer: Lucie Haskins
Design: Patricia Escabi

T.F.H. Publications, Inc.
One TFH Plaza
Third and Union Avenues
Neptune City, NJ 07753

T.F.H. Publications
President/CEO: Glen S. Axelrod
Executive Vice President: Mark E. Johnson
Publisher: Christopher T. Reggio
Production Manager: Kathy Bontz

Library of Congress Cataloging-in-Publication Data
Ewing, Susan M.
  Pembroke Welsh corgi / Susan M. Ewing.
    p. cm. – (Breed lover's guides)
  Includes bibliographical references and index.
  ISBN 978-0-7938-4177-6 (alk. paper)
  1. Pembroke Welsh corgi. I. Title.
  SF429.P33E939 2011
  636.737–dc22
                                        2010004258

The Leader In Responsible Animal Care For Over 50 Years!®
www.tfh.com

Table of Contents

Chapter
1

History of the
Pembroke Welsh Corgi

There are two different types of Welsh Corgis, and they are distinct breeds, not variations. The Cardigan Welsh Corgi is the older of the two and is a larger dog, with ancestral ties to the Dachshund. In fact, early in its development, the Cardigan had drop ears. The Pembroke Welsh Corgi, although a younger breed, has still been around for more than a thousand years and is descended from the spitz, or Northern family of dogs.

The Pembroke Welsh Corgi has been around for more than a thousand years.

The History of the Dog

Of course, all dogs, no matter what the breed, can trace their ancestry back to wolves. Bruce Fogle, in *The Encyclopedia of the Dog* (Dorling Kindersley, 1995) goes back two million years, which is when "the foundation stock for all modern carnivores had evolved," but most people consider the history of the dog to have begun around 15,000 years ago, with evidence of interaction between canines and humans. Everyone seems to agree that *Canis lupus*, the wolf, in one form or another, is the ancestor of all of the breeds of *Canis familiaris*, which is pretty amazing when you consider that the American Kennel Club (AKC) alone recognizes a great number breeds and varieties, and worldwide there are more than 400 specific breeds.

Dog Groups

Richard and Alice Feinnes, in their book *The Natural History of Dogs* (Natural History Press, 1970), place dogs into four groups, depending on which wolf they consider the breed's ancestor. The Asian wolf is behind what they call the Dingo group, which includes the Basenji, Rhodesian Ridgeback, and several European breeds. The Greyhound group springs from a relative of the Asian wolf and includes all of the breeds that are considered sighthounds. Breeds in the Mastiff group trace their origins to the

WHAT IS A BREED CLUB?

On the most basic level, a breed club is a club devoted to just one dog breed. The club works to promote the breed, increase understanding through education, and may have a rescue component. The club may also sponsor conformation shows or performance events limiting entries to the specific breed. A club can be local, regional, or national. Breed clubs are a good way to learn more about a specific breed, as well as function as a place to meet others who love your breed. Regional clubs generally cover several states and are also frequently affiliated with the national club, but they don't have to be.

National clubs are the clubs generally recognized by the American Kennel Club (AKC) as having the authority to write and make changes to the official breed standard. Some national clubs are formed to promote new or rare breeds, and these clubs keep breeding and show records and help get their breed recognized by the AKC. The Pembroke Welsh Corgi Club of America (PWCCA) is the national club for Pems. This organization, like most national clubs, has a website and lists member breeders. This is a good way to find breeders in your area, and while it's not a guarantee of quality, breeders who are a member of the national club subscribe to a code of ethics and have an interest in the breed beyond breeding puppies for a quick buck. The club's website (www. pembrokecorgi.org) can also steer you toward regional clubs and rescue operations. The national club also holds an annual "specialty" show—that is, a show just for Pembroke Welsh Corgis. Nationals are a great way to see hundreds of Corgis all in one location and to meet many breeders and owners.

Breed clubs may also offer special awards to high-achieving dogs of their specific breed. For instance, the Mayflower Pembroke Welsh Corgi Club offers the Lila Wolfman Achievement Award to dogs who have earned a conformation championship, a Companion Dog title in obedience, and a title in another performance event, such as herding or agility.

Tibetan wolf. The Northern wolf is behind many of the so-called northern breeds, as well as the spitz family, which includes the Pembroke Welsh Corgi.

How Dogs Developed From Wolves

Exactly how the dog developed from the wolf is still being debated. One theory is

Exactly how the dog developed from the wolf is still a matter of debate.

that wolf cubs were taken from their dens and raised with humans, but Raymond and Lorna Coppinger, in their book *Dogs: A New Understanding of Canine Origin, Behavior and Evolution* (Scribner, 2001) refute that idea. They claim that, while wolf cubs might indeed have played with humans, as they matured they would leave for the wild. What were needed were wolves that had a tendency to be tame—wolves with shorter flight distances. In other words, wolves who let humans get a bit closer before they ran away. The Coppingers cite Dmitri Belyaev, a Russian who selected for tameness in wild foxes, and in just 18 generations, got not only tame foxes but foxes with dog-like traits. These foxes had tails that curled up on the end, floppy ears, piebald coats, and they barked.

The Coppingers contend that this is the same sort of thing that happened to wolves with shorter flight distances. As people started to settle and practice agriculture, as opposed to being nomadic, wolves were drawn to village dumps. Those wolves with shorter flight distances—that is, those who allowed humans to get closer before they ran away—got more food. Gradually, those wolves with shorter and shorter flight distances got more and more of the food. The wolves that didn't flee could turn the extra calories they gained into producing pups, which in turn reflected the shorter flight distance of their parents. Because the food from the village dumps was generally lower-quality food than what wolves would get from a wild kill, the animals' heads, brains, and teeth became smaller. And because they were living on supplied food, the smaller heads and

As people started to settle and practice agriculture, it's possible that wolves were drawn to village dumps.

BREED HISTORY

— Julia Clough of Sippiwisset Corgis has been breeding Corgis
since 1965. She has put championships on more than 33 of her Corgis,
and her dogs have completed more performance titles than she can count.

Q: How important is the breed's history when you breed? Very few Corgis herd for a living anymore, so does it matter that they were once herding dogs?

A: Herding is what these dogs are. That herding instinct is what makes a Corgi a Corgi—it's what we like about them. We like them because of their heritage. Without that instinct and that heritage, there's no difference between a Corgi and a "designer breed." It is a huge thrill to see your pet dog go in with livestock and see that dog do what he was bred to do. It can bring tears to your eyes. On a personal level, I put herding titles on all of my Corgis.

teeth were not a detriment. They didn't need more intelligence and bigger teeth to hunt and kill prey.

From the generic dog of the dumps grew the many different breeds of today, starting, in all probability, with guard dogs, and with dogs that, by extension, helped guard herds of grazing animals. According to *The Complete Book of the Dog* edited by David Macdonald, there are records of hunting dogs existing in Egypt 6,000 years ago, and in *Old Farm Dogs*, author David Hancock cites a fresco dating to 2000 BCE that shows herding dogs.

The Early Pembroke Welsh Corgi

So we have some herding dogs 2,000 years ago, and now we need to get to the Pembroke Welsh Corgi. Because

specific breeds with carefully recorded pedigrees didn't become popular until the 1800s, there's no way of knowing when the Pembroke Welsh Corgi, as we know him, definitely came into being. The 10th century used to be the best guess for the first Corgi-type dogs, but in 2004, a team of archaeologists excavating a royal dwelling in the Brecon Beacons of South Wales found the bones of a Corgi-sized dog. They estimate that the site was inhabited around 890 CE.

Herding dogs are mentioned in the laws of Hywel Dda (Howell the Good), who ruled in Wales from 904 to 950 CE. Under the heading, "The Value of Wild and Tame," there is this: "A dunghill cur, to whomsoever it belongs (even if it belongs to the King), its value is fourpence. A herding dog, however, which guards the stock and goes before them in the morning and comes home behind them at night, is worth the most important beast of the stock he guards." Although the size of the herding dog is not mentioned, it's a good guess that some of these dogs were Corgi sized.

Recognition of Breed Type

Fast forward a few hundred years, and we find recognition of breed type in this quote from *A General History of Quadrupeds*, by Thomas Bewick, written in 1790: "The Cur Dog is a trusty and useful servant to the farmer and grazier; and…such great attention paid in breeding it, that we cannot help considering it as a permanent kind… They are chiefly employed in driving cattle…They bite very keenly; and as they always make their attack at the heels, the cattle have no defence against them." In Spurrell's Welsh dictionary of 1859, the meaning of "Corgi" was given as cur-dog from either Cur-ci or Cor-ci, with "ci" translating as dog and "cor" as dwarf. "The corgi-type heelers have to be agile, quick, and alert, if only to survive. As cattle dogs, they have to learn to bite the hind foot that is bearing weight, giving them that extra split second to duck or flatten to avoid the reacting hefty kick. They learn, too, to attack alternate feet, rather than repeating their first attempt, in order to cause a little more surprise."

Spurrell's translation of the name "Corgi" to mean "dwarf dog" is the most popular interpretation of the name. "Dwarf" in Welsh is *Corrach*, so it's possible that a contraction of that word formed "Corgi." One source suggests that "Cor" translates to "to watch over, or gather." I love this suggestion but can't find anything to support its accuracy.

Corgi Ancestry

Likely suspects of Corgi ancestry include

Likely Corgi ancestors include the Swedish Valhund, pictured here, among others.

There's no way to know positively what breeds went into the making of the Pembroke Welsh Corgi.

the Swedish Valhund, the Norwegian Buhund, and the Lundehund. Norsemen raided the Welsh coast in the 9th and 10th centuries; they may have had dogs aboard their ships, and they may as well have possibly taken Welsh dogs home with them. It's possible that these dogs had an influence on the dog who eventually became the Pembroke Welsh Corgi. Flemish weavers who immigrated to Wales in the 11th and 12th centuries

may have introduced the Schipperke to their new homeland, thus adding another northern breed to the mix.

What are these possible ancestors like? Well, the Lundehund of Norway measures 12.5 to 14.5 inches (31.5 to 37 cm) tall, just a bit taller than modern Corgis. They are brown, with black tipping on each hair and some white markings. They have prick ears and are double jointed, as well as having extra toes for more efficiently being able to climb rocks as they hunt for puffins. This kind of hunting dog would have been useful to the Norsemen on their costal raids, as they could hunt puffins for food. Modern Corgis don't have extra toes or such flexible joints, but with some other breeds thrown in, there's no way to rule out a dash of Lundehund blood.

The Buhund is another Norwegian breed that may also have contributed to the Corgi. It stands 17 to 18 inches (43 to 45.5 cm) tall and weighs 26 to 40 pounds (12 to 18 kg); it was originally a herding dog. They come in wheaten, black, and sable and may have white markings and/ or a black mask. According to Bonnie Wilcox and Chris Walkowicz in *The Atlas of Dog Breeds of the World*, "Buhunds are clean, intelligent, and fun. They also have the northern traits of great energy, the desire for human companionship, and the need for a firm, consistent master to overcome their strong will." That certainly

TIMELINE

- 2000 BCE: A fresco created in that year depicts herding dogs.
- 890 CE: Dogs similar to the modern-day Pembroke Welsh Corgi are part of a royal Welsh household.
- 1086: Corgi mentioned in Welsh Doomsday book.
- 1925: First Corgi shown at a dog show
- 1925: The Welsh Corgi Club founded in Great Britain.
- 1933: The Duke of York (later, King George VI) gives a Corgi puppy to his daughters, Elizabeth and Margaret. They call the puppy "Dookie."
- 1934: The Kennel Club (Britain) separates Pembroke and Cardigan Welsh Corgis into two separate breeds.
- 1934: Little Madam becomes the first Pembroke Welsh Corgi to be registered with the American Kennel Club (AKC).
- 1935: The American Kennel Club acknowledges the two separate breeds, Pembroke and Cardigan, with the registration of Cardigan Welsh Corgi Blodwen of Robinscroft.
- 1936: The Pembroke Welsh Corgi Club of America is founded.
- 1944: Princess Elizabeth receives a Corgi for her eighteenth birthday. All of the royal Corgis are descended from this Corgi, Susan. In 2009, the queen owned four Corgis: Linnet, Monty, Willow, and Holly.
- 1983: Author gets her first (but not last!) Corgi puppy.
- 2000: Ch. Coventry Queue wins the herding group at the Westminster Kennel Club Dog Show.
- 2001: "Queue" repeats the win.
- 2002: Ch. Shafrhaus Sammy Sosa wins the Herding Group at the Westminster Kennel Club Dog Show.
- 2004: Ch. Hum'nbird Keepin Up'pearances wins the Herding Group at the Westminster Kennel Club Dog Show.
- 2008: The American Kennel Club lists the Pembroke Welsh Corgi as 24th in popularity out of 160 different breeds and varieties.

When the Lancashire Heeler almost became extinct, Corgis and the Manchester Terrier (pictured here) were used to recreate the breed.)

closer to 45 pounds (20.5 kg), with much longer fur, but its longer fur may have contributed to the "fluffy" gene in Corgis.

A British dog may also have contributed to the making of the Corgi. David Hancock, in *Old Farm Dogs*, suggests that the Lancashire Heeler could have helped to create the Corgi. According to Deborah Harper, in her book *The New Complete Pembroke Welsh Corgi*, Corgi breeder Eve Forsyth-Forrest also believed in the connection to the Lancashire Heeler. "At the time of the Saxon invasions, some Britons fled into the depths of the Forest of Elmet, and it was there a pocket of their Corgi-like Lancashire Heelers survived the passing centuries." In an odd twist, the original Lancashire Heeler became almost extinct, and Corgis and Manchester Terriers have been used to help recreate this ancient breed.

There's no way to know positively what breeds went into the making of the Pembroke Welsh Corgi. There may have been a connection to all of the breeds mentioned or to only one or two—but the result is what's important, and that result was an energetic, intelligent dog who, because of his size, didn't require much food or space on the early Welsh farms but could make himself useful in many areas. Traditionally, Pembroke Welsh Corgis were used to move stock from one place to another. Although known as a herding dog, which he certainly was,

sounds like a Corgi!

The Swedish Valhund weighs 20 to 32 (9 to 14.5 kg) pounds and stands 13 to 16 inches (33 to 40.5 cm) tall. This dog looks a lot like a Corgi, but there seems to be a question as to whether the Valhund traveled to Wales or the Corgi traveled to Sweden.

The Finish Lapphund is taller yet, at 18 to 20 inches (45.5 to 51 cm), and weighs especially when it came to cattle and geese, the Pembroke Welsh Corgi was also useful as a ratter in the barn and could even retrieve fallen game.

The Corgi Today

While there were probably a few Pembroke Welsh Corgis in the United States before 1934, Little Madam was the first Pembroke Welsh Corgi registered with the AKC in 1934. Mrs. Lewis Roesler, who was known at the time for her Old English Sheepdogs, bought Little Madam in England and brought her to the United States. At the time of her registration, she was recorded as a Welsh Corgi, but by 1935, the AKC recognized the Cardigan and the Pembrokes as two separate breeds. Little Madam was a daughter of Bowhit Pepper, who passed on his good genes to his progeny.

The Corgi today owes much to the early Corgi fanciers and their breeding programs. Many Corgis in both conformation and performance events can trace their ancestry to kennels in the United Kingdom. Bowhit, Stormerbanks, Hildenmanor, Blands, Lees, and Belroyd kennels produced generations of quality Corgis. On this side of the Atlantic, Cote de Neige kennels had a huge influence, along with Larklain, Nebriowa, Festiniog, and Schaferhaus kennels.

Breeders today continue the practice of breeding "the best to the best" with the help of science, utilizing DNA testing as well as tests to ensure that their breeding stock is free of eye problems and hip dysplasia. Temperament is another important part of the Corgi package, and today's Corgis are as alert, friendly, and intelligent as their great-great-grandparents.

The energetic Pembroke Welsh Corgi makes a wonderful family pet, as well as being an eager partner in whatever activities his owner might enjoy, from fetching a stick or ball, to herding, to competing in obedience, agility, tracking, or conformation. Some Corgis still end up on farms, helping with livestock and vermin control.

Chapter
2

Characteristics of Your Pembroke Welsh Corgi

The Pembroke Welsh Corgi is a short, compact dog, in keeping with what Welsh farmers needed hundreds of years ago. There wasn't a lot of extra food for feeding a large dog, and they also needed a dog who could do more than herd their cattle. They needed a dog who could also catch vermin and who could sound the alarm if there were intruders. The Corgi fit the bill, being brave and agile and possessing the bark of a much larger dog.

Like all purebreds, the parent club has written a *breed standard*, the standard by which the dog should be judged in a show ring. A Corgi may not meet the standard but still be an excellent pet. However, if you think that you'd like to show your dog, study the standard. You'll find the official standard on the Pembroke Welsh Corgi Club of America's (PWCCA) website at www.pembrokecorgi.org.

Physical Characteristics of the Corgi

The general picture of a Corgi shows short, fairly straight legs (the front legs curve around the chest slightly); a fox-like head, including erect ears; and a docked tail.

Size

Corgis are longer than they are tall but are not so long, in proportion to their height, as a Dachshund. Typically, a Corgi is about 12 inches (30.5 cm) tall at the withers and about 16 or 17 inches (40.5 to 43 cm) from the withers to the tail. Corgis weigh between 25 and 27 pounds (11.5 and 12 kg), but you may find a Corgi closer to 22 pounds (10 kg) or weighing as much as 30 pounds (13.5 kg). Anything over or under those figures is likely to be too light boned and delicate looking or very heavy and unlikely to have the agility and stamina that would be required to herd livestock.

The Pembroke Welsh Corgi is a short, compact dog.

Puppy Love

PUPPY TROUBLE

Puppies have the same characteristics as adults, but more so. They will get into everything and love to explore, so make sure that your home is puppy-proofed. One good way to do this is to get down on your hands and knees and look at things from a dog's-eye view. An electrical cord can be irresistible to an inquisitive puppy, and it can also be deadly. Keep wires close to the wall or run them through a length of PVC pipe.

Move breakables and treasured books to a shelf that your puppy can't reach. To a Corgi puppy, there's nothing more fun than gnawing on the spine of a book. The same goes for insecticides and household cleaning products. Make sure that your puppy can't get into kitchen cupboards, either. Many food products, such as chocolate, raisins, onions, and macadamia nuts, can be harmful, if not fatal, to dogs.

Puppies are like toddlers. They will put just about anything in their mouths as they learn about their environment. Pick up small items that might cause choking, or might, if swallowed, cause an intestinal blockage.

Put a baby gate at the tops of flights of stairs, and make sure that the door to the basement is kept closed. Puppies can be a bit clumsy and may not be able to manage a flight of stairs at first.

Your puppy will play hard and will then need a nap, so give him time to recharge those batteries.

Head
Corgis have black noses, lips, and eye rims, and their teeth meet in a scissors bite. Having an overshot or undershot jaw would prevent them from doing their job of nipping at the ankles of cattle or catching mice and rats. Their muzzle is fairly long but not as long and pointy as, say, a Borzoi's. There is a well-defined stop, which is the place where the muzzle joins the rest of the head. The skull is flat between the ears.

When looked at from the front, the tips of the ears, and the nose should form an equilateral triangle.

Chest, Rib Cage, and Topline
Corgis have a deep chest, allowing for plenty of lung and heart room. The breastbone is prominent in front, and the chest is below the elbows, which are held close to the body. The rib cage is egg-shaped. The topline, or back, is level.

Feet

Corgis have compact feet, with the two middle toes extending just slightly in front of the outside toes. The front legs should not turn either in or out, and the back legs, seen from the rear, show straight, strong hocks.

Tail

A Corgi may be born with a naturally short tail, but most are surgically docked at the same time that the dewclaws are removed, at the age of three days. Many European countries now prohibit docking, so we may see more Corgis with tails in the future. Because tail set has never been bred for, there is currently no uniformity. The tail may curl up over the back, which is typical of breeds of northern ancestry.

Coat

Corgis have a thick double coat, consisting of a fluffy, soft undercoat, and a harsher outercoat. This keeps them warm and dry in almost all weather and provides the Corgi owner with an endless supply of dust bunnies made of dog hair. Corgis supposedly shed heavily twice a year, and it's true that the spring shed can produce an amazing amount of fur, but in reality, Corgis shed all year long. Females also tend to lose undercoat just after they have been in season. A side benefit to spaying your female is that you won't have

Corgis have a thick double coat that consists of a fluffy undercoat and a harsher outercoat.

that shedding to contend with.

The coat should be straight, although a very slight wave is allowed by the standard. The coat is thick but should be fairly short. A Corgi with long fur, like a Shetland Sheepdog's, is called a "fluffy." The first sign that a puppy is a fluffy is long, soft hair around the ears. As the dog grows, the fur gets longer and longer. Adult fluffies look a bit like an animated haystack. While the fluffy coat is a fault in the show ring, many people like the long, soft fur and would rather have a fluffy than a dog with the correct coat. If that's your preference, be prepared for much more grooming, because that long, soft hair can mat easily, and of course, there'll be much more shedding.

Coat Colors

Corgis can come in a variety of colors, with or without white markings, and they are all acceptable. The red of a red Corgi can range from a light fawn to a deep red. Sable Corgis have an overlay of black hairs on top of the red. Black-headed tricolors are black with tan "eyebrows," tan on the cheeks, and under the tail. There may also be tan on the legs. A black or black-and-white Corgi without tan points is not an acceptable color combination according to the official standard. A redheaded tricolor is marked a bit like a Beagle, with a black saddle, tan legs, and tan head, with or without white markings. The black area may cover the neck and back or be a smaller saddle.

Occasionally, a Corgi will have a steel blue, or gray, coat. These are called "blueies," and this is a very serious fault. A blueie's nose, lips, and eye rims will be gray, rather than the desired black. Another serious fault is a "whitely," which means that the dog has a predominantly white coat with colored patches. Mismarked coats are also a fault.

CORGIS AND KIDS

If puppies and children go together like peanut butter and jelly, then Corgi puppies and children go together like, well—like even more peanut butter and jelly! Corgis enjoy attention and play and are sturdy enough, even as puppies, to tolerate a certain amount of roughhousing. That's not to say that they shouldn't be treated with care, but they are not as fragile as some toy breeds. Even as puppies, most will try to retrieve a toy. Letting children play with your Corgi is a wonderful way to socialize a puppy, as well as help him burn off excess energy and get exercise, but that play should always be supervised.

Make sure your that the puppy still gets his nap breaks. Also, make sure that all of the children know the puppy-handling rules: no pulling legs or ears or dragging the puppy around, and no hitting. Teach children how to hold and carry a puppy, or if the children are very young, forbid carrying and encourage the children to sit on the floor to play with the puppy. If play starts to get too rough or the children or the puppy are getting overexcited, call a time-out so that everyone can calm down. Never leave even a puppy alone with a baby.

Corgis may have white on their feet and legs, on their faces, and on their necks, either as a full collar or as a white patch, but there should be no white on their bodies above the line of the elbow.

Living With a Corgi

More important than the physical attributes of a Corgi is the breed's personality. That personality can make you ignore all of those dust bunnies!

Your Corgi needs to be socialized to children.

General Temperament

Corgis are bright, alert, curious little dogs, and while there are variations among individuals, they are friendly and outgoing. They make good watchdogs in that they will tell you if there's someone at the door (or if a leaf has fallen), but once that person is inside, they will generally accept her as a friend. On a walk, they will politely say hello to other pedestrians and allow themselves to be petted, but then they'll be just as happy to move on.

A Corgi is happiest with a job to do. You don't need a herd of cattle or a flock of ducks, but that busy, intelligent mind needs to be occupied. Herding, obedience, rally, and agility are all good activities, as is tracking. If you're not into organized activities, most Corgis will be happy to retrieve a tennis ball for as long as you care to throw it. Buy a variety of toys for your Corgi and rotate them so that he always has something new to think about. There are also puzzle games made for dogs, and these can give your Corgi some mental exercise as well.

Remember that your average Corgi will happily take a mile if given the inch. If you let that adorable puppy cuddle with you on the couch or in your bed, expect to find him there when he's an adult as well. If you don't want him on the furniture, he can learn that, but even just one time on that soft sofa, and he'll consider it his right. Corgis are quick learners, and that means that they can learn bad habits as easily as good ones.

Companionability
Socialized properly, Corgis are excellent with children and generally good with other dogs and with cats.

With Children
Although a Corgi's temperament has a lot to do with his ability to get along with kids, Corgis also need training and socialization. Your Corgi may be inclined to be good around children, but if he never sees a child, he may be fearful, which in turn could lead to barking and snapping. If you have children, make sure that they understand how to behave around a dog. Teach older children how to properly pick up a puppy. Have younger children sit down to hold the puppy. Puppies are great wigglers and can get seriously injured if they are dropped.

Ears and legs are not to be tugged and pulled, and your puppy should be allowed to eat and sleep undisturbed. If you don't have children, invite neighbor children to visit your puppy. Take walks around the neighborhood and encourage supervised petting. Malls are good places to meet all kinds of people, both adults and children. You probably can't take your dog into the mall, but just walking around the outside of the building, you'll come in contact with lots of people. Carry a pocketful of

Corgis also must be socialized to other dogs.

treats and ask people you meet to give a treat to your puppy. Soon he'll associate strangers with good things.

As good as your adult dog may be around children, never, ever leave any dog unattended with a baby. Babies make high-pitched noises, and that, combined with jerky movements, can make the baby seem like prey to your dog. Supervise interactions between toddlers and dogs as well. Toddlers can be too rough, and if the child is indeed a toddler and unsteady when walking, a tumble could accidentally hurt your puppy or dog.

Ask the Expert

IMPORTANT BREEDING QUESTIONS

—Julia Clough, Corgi breeder

Q: What characteristics are most important to you when breeding?

A: I breed for health and temperament because 99 percent of my puppies go as pets, but it's a package. Health and temperament lead it, but there are lots of beautiful dogs, so there's no reason why you can't have a beautiful dog and still have good health and temperament. Also, I like the conformation of a working dog. Some breeders, who breed only for the show ring, have produced Corgis who are too long, too low, and too heavy. I believe that Corgis were originally a small dog, and I try to keep that balance. I want a dog who is hardy and who can run and jump and herd, as well as look good.

Q: Do you perform health checks?

A: Yes. I only breed dogs who are cleared for von Willebrand's disease; I won't breed carriers. Eyes need to be clear, and I X-ray hips. I believe nutrition helps as far as having good hips. I like to give my puppies V-8 juice for vitamins, rather than supplements. The dogs I breed must be absolutely sound, which means that they must have good movement.

With Dogs

If you bring home your Corgi as a puppy and you already have another dog, supervise their first meeting—just in case—but you shouldn't have any problems. If you're adopting an older dog, use a bit more caution. Introduce the dogs on neutral ground if that's possible. If not, at least make the introductions out in the yard. Have both dogs on lead but try to keep the leads slack. A tight lead brings a dog's head up in an aggressive position, plus the tension on the lead can signal to your dog that there's a problem. Feed the dogs in separate locations, and for the first week or so, try not to leave any toys or bones around that might cause an argument.

As far as other dogs go, you'll have to see how your own Corgi reacts. Most of mine have been good around other dogs, but my current male has always wanted to attack bigger dogs, like Wolfhounds or German Shepherd Dogs. Heavy emphasis on socialization should go a long way toward making your Corgi a good citizen.

Companionability With Cats

Corgis as a breed seem to get along very well with cats. If you are bringing a puppy into a home with a resident cat, let them get to know each other slowly. Crate the puppy, or put him in an exercise pen and let the cat make the first approach. Once the cat has accepted the puppy, always make sure that the cat has somewhere to escape to if the puppy starts getting too rambunctious. Baby gates in doorways are a good way to contain a puppy, and most cats can easily jump back and forth. Once the puppy is older, make sure that there's a shelf or ledge where the cat can get away from canine attentions. If you're bringing an adult Corgi home, use caution, especially if the cat isn't used to dogs. A friendly advance by your Corgi could be met with slashing claws. Take it slowly, and again, make sure that the cat has an escape route.

With Other Pets

As far as other types of pets are concerned, if you have a rabbit, guinea pig, gerbil, or hamster, keep them safely away from your Corgi. There are many stories about dogs getting along with mice or curling up happily with the family rabbit, but generally, your Corgi is apt to look upon these small, furry animals as lunch. Use caution and keep your "pocket pets" out of harm's way.

Environment

Whether you live in a big city high-rise, a residential neighborhood, or out on a farm, your Corgi will easily adapt to that environment. A Corgi is a compact little dog, so he can easily live in an apartment, but if you have a fenced yard in the suburbs, he'll enjoy that, and if you're on a farm, he'll be in heaven. The main things to remember are that Corgis do need some exercise, and they need to be with their people. That doesn't mean that if you're gone most of the day you shouldn't have a Corgi, but it does mean that if that's the case, you need to give your dog some quality time—and that means not only physical exercise but some mental stimulation as well.

Exercise

As far as exercise goes, if you live in the city, a brisk walk twice a day, with shorter walks in between will work just fine. If you have a fenced yard, your Corgi can get exercise playing with children or another dog or retrieving a ball. He probably won't get much exercise in a yard unless he does have a playmate. Just because you don't have to walk your dog doesn't mean that you shouldn't. Rural living doesn't mean opening the door and letting your Corgi run, but it can mean supervised exercise, or if you have some livestock, maybe your Corgi's herding instinct will come out and he can help you with chores, as well as getting his exercise.

Regardless of where you live, if you're interested in any of the performance events, a bit of daily practice will help

Whether you live on a farm or in a high-rise or residential neighborhood, your Corgi will easily adapt to that environment.

your Corgi get the exercise he needs, as well as offer mental stimulation and some quality time with you.

Nipping

Corgis generally have pleasant temperaments, but they are a herding breed, and so nipping at heels comes naturally. They enjoy the chase, and instinct tells them to bite at the heels of whatever they're chasing. If children are running around in your yard, your Corgi will want to chase them and will probably nip. This is not to be confused with aggressive biting. You can teach a Corgi not to do this, but it's a bit like trying to teach a terrier not to dig. Teach your children to stop running, and try to distract your Corgi with a toy. Or you may just need to take your Corgi in the house when the yard is full of children.

Trainability

Whether or not you plan to pursue any formal activities, your Corgi puppy will need some training. Cute puppy antics

Characteristics Checklist

When buying a puppy

✓ Look for a dog with clear eyes and no nasal discharge.
✓ A puppy may show various levels of energy, but should not be limp or lethargic.
✓ Ask for proof of vaccinations.
✓ Ask about health clearances (have the parents been tested for von Willebrand's disease, hip dysplasia, eye diseases?)
✓ Get registration papers (American Kennel Club [AKC] or United Kennel Club, or if your dog is Canadian, Canadian Kennel Club [CKC]. These are the three best-known).
✓ Ask for at least a three-generation pedigree, especially if you plan to show or compete in performance events.
✓ There should be a contract between you and your breeder. Read and understand it before you sign.

aren't so cute in an adult dog, and all dogs need to be taught basic manners or they're not much fun to be around. Definitely start training when your Corgi is a puppy. That way, he is learning the correct way to behave, rather than doing things his way and having to be retaught later. It's much easier to train proper behavior than to try to change a bad habit. The good news about training a Corgi is that they learn quickly and seem to enjoy it. Remember to keep your training sessions short, as puppies don't have a long attention span. Two or three 5-minute sessions are better than one 15-minute session.

Corgis learn quickly, but that's not to say they will always obey. They frequently think for themselves, and if they think they know a better way, they'll try it. Or if

they think that they're doing something the right way, it can be very hard to convince them that your way is better.

Water

Corgi puppies, especially, enjoy splashing in water. We always had a large water bowl, purchased originally to accommodate our large mixed breed. All of our Corgi puppies over the years found it a wonderful wading pool. They loved putting their front paws in the dish and paddling, especially if they were warm after a play session. It's great fun to watch. Invest in a bowl that doesn't tip over, put a large bath towel under it, and enjoy.

Chapter
3

Supplies for Your
Pembroke Welsh Corgi

You've chosen your Corgi, but before you bring your puppy or adult dog home, you'll need to do some shopping. Although your shopping list may seem long, many of the items will last the lifetime of your Corgi—and beyond. Some items you might even find at a garage sale, or check to see if your local humane society has a thrift shop.

Wherever you shop, don't skimp on quality. A crate with rough edges or a bad door catch, or a leash that snaps when you're out for a walk is no bargain and may put your puppy's life in danger.

Baby Gate

Baby gates make it easy to confine your puppy in a specific room while still allowing air to circulate and making it possible to hear your puppy. Most adult humans can step over these gates, or they are easily removed from the doorway. Baby gates also give the family cat a way to escape a puppy's attentions.

Bed

Dozens of different types of dog beds are on the market, so personal taste

You may have to wait until your Corgi is an adult before you get him that special bed.

is going to be your determining factor. Something soft to cushion adult dogs is a good idea, and the outer shell should be washable. If that outer layer has also been treated to help repel liquids, so much the better. Whatever type of bed you like, you might want to wait until your puppy is an adult before buying that special bed. Corgis housetrain easily but may still have the occasional accident in the crate, and they also like to chew. Even surrounded by wonderful chew toys, your puppy may prefer the expensive bed.

For the first year or so, make a bed of old towels. You can give your puppy several layers for softness and warmth. The towels will wash and dry quickly, and you won't mind if your puppy chews a few holes in them. Once your puppy is over the teething stage, you can shop for that elegant four-poster with the innerspring mattress.

Collar

You will need a collar (and leash) for your Corgi. Puppies grow quickly, so don't invest in a fancy leather collar right away. Get your puppy used to wearing a thin nylon collar. The best is the kind where the tongue of the buckle just

Check It Out

SUPPLIES CHECKLIST

There are all kinds of pet-related products you can buy, but get the basics first:

✓ bed (or stock up on towels for the first year)

✓ collar and lead

✓ crate

✓ food and water bowls (stainless steel is best)

✓ grooming tools (at least a comb and nail clippers)

✓ some form of identification (or more than one)

✓ toothbrush and toothpaste

✓ toys

pushes through the nylon, making it easily adjustable as your puppy grows.

Once your dog is an adult, you can buy a permanent collar. Nylon is a fine choice, and if you select a nylon lead as well, you can color coordinate the two. Nylon wears well and can be washed. Leather collars are more expensive but will last forever and look good. Rolled leather collars help prevent flattening the fur.

Whether you're fitting a puppy collar or an adult collar, you should be able to slide two fingers between the collar and the dog's neck. Much looser, and your dog may be able to paw the collar off. Much tighter, and if your dog gains a bit of weight, the collar can start to choke him. Also, a tight collar doesn't allow you to slide your hand under it if you need to restrain your dog.

Crate

One of the first things on the puppy shopping list is a crate. Some people may look at a crate and think "cage," and from there, they think "cruel." But used properly, a crate can be a wonderful training tool and can also provide your puppy—and later, your adult dog—with a safe haven. A crate helps keep your puppy safe when you can't watch him, and it offers a cozy place to sleep. Because no dog wants to go to the bathroom where he sleeps, a crate can also help you housetrain your Corgi.

Crates are made of various materials. Whatever type you purchase, it should be big enough for your dog to stretch out when lying down, and your dog should be able to easily turn around in it. A dog should also be able to stand up in his crate, but with Corgis, headroom isn't usually a problem.

Once you've realized how useful a crate can be, you may want to buy more than one. You can use one for the car, one in your bedroom, one in the family room, and maybe even one for travel.

Wire Crates

Wire crates generally have a removable tray for easy cleaning and are lightweight. The disadvantage is that they are not particularly warm and cozy. Drape a towel or blanket over this type of crate to provide a shelter from drafts. In hot weather, the sides of the

Used properly, a crate can be a wonderful training tool.

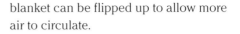

blanket can be flipped up to allow more air to circulate.

Plastic Crates

Airline crates are generally made of heavy-duty plastic. These crates are good for travel, and they come apart for easy cleaning. They can be hotter in summer, though, than a wire crate.

Mesh Crates

Travel crates typically collapse for easy handling. I have two lightweight mesh crates that collapse for travel and are perfect for taking into a motel room. These crates are not good for puppies who like to chew or dig, or for adult dogs who may also want to escape. They work best for calm adult dogs.

Wooden and Wicker Crates

If you'd like a crate to accent your decor, wooden crates are available, as well as attractive wicker models. These generally cost more than the plainer models. Some people create crate covers to match draperies or bedspreads.

Ex-Pen

You might also want an exercise pen, abbreviated ex-pen. These wire pens fold up for storage, and in addition to being made into a pen, can be used stretched out to block off

Your Corgi may benefit from using an ex-pen.

a porch or an archway between rooms. Pop your puppy in an ex-pen, and he can enjoy the yard while you garden, and you'll know right where he is.

Food and Water Bowls

Ideally, you want bowls that are sturdy enough so that they can't easily be tipped over by your puppy. Whatever your choice, buy bowls that fit your dog's size. A Corgi doesn't need a 2-quart (2-L) bowl for food. Having said that, I would recommend a larger bowl for water. This isn't because Corgi puppies drink more than other dogs; it's because they love to play in the water. Corgis understand

the connection between cooling off and water, and after a play session, your puppy may head for the water bowl, put both front feet in, and start paddling, splashing water on his stomach, and of course, all over your kitchen floor. Yes, it's a mess,

Stainless steel is an excellent choice for your Corgi's food and water bowls.

Puppy Love

PUPPY AND ADULT DOG SUPPLIES

Puppies and adults both need the same things: dishes, toys, beds, crates, collars, and leads. Puppies generally need a smaller size in everything than an adult Corgi. So if you don't have a small puppy crate, consider putting a divider in an adult-sized crate. Many wire crates come with a divider panel, and this can make housetraining easier because the puppy can't use one end of an adult crate as a bedroom and the other end as a bathroom. Generally, Corgis housetrain very quickly, but the smaller the crate, the better for those first couple of months.

An adult lead will probably work just fine, but an adult collar is not going to work on your puppy. Inexpensive nylon collars are your best bet.

Corgis puppies are willing to tackle adult-sized toys, but if you do buy smaller toys, make sure to replace them as your puppy grows. A toy that was just right two weeks ago may now be small enough to swallow or to choke on. Too big a toy is preferable to too small.

but it's guaranteed to bring a smile, and you can always put a large bath towel under the bowl. Another choice for water is a large water cooler-type dispenser. A large bottle of water fills a smaller attached bowl, keeping the water fresher. There are also pet water bowls that offer a constant supply of running water.

During the hot summer months, consider investing in a kiddy wading pool. Just a few inches (cm) of water in the pool can mean cool fun for your Corgi.

Ceramic

Ceramic bowls can be a good choice, and they frequently come in cute doggy designs. They can be popped into the dishwasher for cleaning. Ceramic dishes are breakable,

however, and, if you do choose ceramic, make sure that the glaze is lead-free.

Plastic

Plastic bowls may be heavy enough, and most are dishwasher-proof in the top rack, but they might be tempting as teething toys, and a scratched and bitten dish offers lots of great hiding places for bacteria. If the plastic is soft enough for your puppy to actually chew off a chunk, there's the risk of him choking. Also, occasionally, a dog can develop acne from having his chin rub against the plastic, although this is more of a problem with short-faced dogs than with Corgis.

Stainless Steel

Stainless steel is an excellent choice. It is chew-proof and unbreakable and can be washed in the dishwasher. Many stainless steel bowls come weighted or with a rubber ring on the bottom to help prevent tipping.

Grooming Supplies

Corgis don't need much grooming, but they do need some, so basic grooming tools should be on your list.

Comb and Slicker Brush

A comb and a slicker brush will help you brush out dead undercoat, and you'll need nail clippers or a grinding tool. A slicker brush has thin wire bristles, bent slightly at the top.

Nail Clippers

Nail clippers come in different styles but whichever kind you prefer, get good ones so that they'll stay sharp. Many Corgis resent having their feet handled and seem

A grooming table is helpful because it saves your back from bending over during a grooming session.

to prefer having their nails ground with a Dremel tool. Talk to your breeder or a groomer about the proper way to use these tools.

Shedding Rake/Rubber Brush

A shedding rake can help when your Corgi is shedding in the spring or fall, and a nubbly rubber brush can help with dead guard hairs, but you can live without either of these.

Grooming Table

A grooming table is also helpful because it puts your Corgi at your level and saves your back during a grooming session, but it's not a necessity.

Toothbrush and Toothpaste

Get in the habit of brushing your dog's teeth. Dogs don't usually get cavities, but they do get plaque and tartar buildup, which can cause problems. Invest in a dog toothbrush and a tube of special doggy toothpaste. (Never use human toothpaste.) Start by wrapping your finger with gauze and gently rubbing your puppy's teeth and gums. Don't force the issue, and always reward him for allowing you to do so. Eventually, you can graduate to a small brush that fits over your finger. Your adult dog should accept a toothbrush. Daily brushing is wonderful; a few times a week is acceptable, and even once a week will help.

Identification

Identification is as important for your dog as it is for you. Should he stray, it can mean the difference between getting your dog back and never having him return home.

Collar Tags

While ID tags on your dog's collar are a good, visible way to let people know that he is a beloved pet, tags can be removed or fall off. If you are using collar tags, consider a cell phone number that is good even if you were traveling, and/or your veterinarian's number. If you don't have a cell phone, consider having a special tag made when you travel that gives the number of the place where you're staying. Your home phone number won't be much

ID tags are a good, visible way to let people know that your dog is a beloved pet.

use if your Corgi gets loose in the middle of New Mexico.

Microchipping

In addition to collar tags, consider microchipping your Corgi. Microchips are about the size of a grain of rice and are inserted by your veterinarian between your dog's shoulder blades. A special scanner can read the information on the chip, which includes an identification number on file with whatever company made your particular chip. The shelter or veterinarian who scans your dog can then contact the company, and it in turn can notify you as to your dog's whereabouts. Generally, shelters and veterinarian offices have a scanner that will read the majority of chips, but it's a good idea to choose a major company to increase the likelihood that your dog's chip will be read by the scanner.

Tattoos

Tattoos are another method of identification. One of my dogs was tattooed by her breeder. The problem is that hair has grown over the tattoo, and also, unless someone reading the tattoo knows what it means (in my case, a Canadian Kennel Club [CKC] number), it's not much help.

Leash

Nylon, cotton, or leather leads are all fine choices, and a 6-foot (2-m) leash is a good length for walks. Get one that fits easily in your hand. My personal preference is leather. I like the look and feel, and leather just gets softer and more flexible the more you use it.

Avoid chain or plastic leads. Plastic doesn't have a long life and is not very flexible, and chain can tear the skin off your hand if your dog makes a sudden leap while you're holding the chain. Many people like retractable leads, which are thin cords housed in a plastic case. These are useful for giving your dog lots of freedom when you are in an open field or any large, uncongested area. Many people get quite good at "reeling" their dog in. The disadvantage is that a longer cord can get easily caught on trees or shrubs, and if you need to get your dog

THE MOST IMPORTANT SUPPLIES

—Julia Clough, Corgi breeder

Q: Is there anything you can't live without? What's the one thing you'd recommend to a first-time puppy owner?

A: A crate is a given. Next, I highly recommend an ex-pen, so then the puppy can be with people wherever they are. Next, a metal food bowl and a slicker brush and Greyhound comb. I like the nubbly nylon bones for chew toys.

back to you quickly, the thin cord can be unpleasant to hold. The retractable lead also allows your dog to get a long way away from you, which can cause problems if another dog approaches. In a crowded area, the cord gets in everyone's way. They're not very useful in training situations either. Get a standard 6-foot (2-m) lead first, and then if a retractable lead will help for exercise in an open area, add that to your shopping list.

Toys

Now comes the fun part. It's time to shop for toys. When it comes to dog toys, there are dozens of choices, and the only thing better than shopping for toys for your puppy is watching him play with those toys. It's not all fun and games, though. You need to think about some things when you're shopping for those toys. First, make sure that the toys are not too small. Better to buy a toy that seems huge in comparison to your puppy than to buy something too small. Too small means that there's a risk of your puppy swallowing the toy, which could lead to intestinal blockage and surgery. Just a bit too small could mean that your puppy could choke to death. Also, puppies grow rapidly, so that tiny ball that was perfect when you brought your puppy home will soon be too small and a danger.

Corgi puppies will tackle and play with just about anything, so go ahead and buy an adult-sized ball and enjoy watching your puppy figure out just how to play with something as large as he is. Balls are always a good choice because Corgis love to chase and retrieve balls. I like tennis balls because they are safer to throw indoors and are soft enough that if an adult Corgi catches one in his mouth, there's little threat of tooth damage. Just remember to remove the ball if your dog decides to just settle down to chew it apart.

Stuffed toys are popular, and puppies especially enjoy curling up for a nap next to, or on top of, stuffed toys, like those Nylabone makes. Supervise play until you know how your Corgi will play with a stuffed toy. I once had a Corgi who just loved carrying a stuffed toy in her mouth. She didn't ever chew it much, and it lasted a long time. She was an exception. All of my other Corgis have felt it was in their job description to disembowel a stuffed toy as quickly as possible. Oh, they may have cuddled a bit as puppies, but once they were a bit older, the goal was to reach the squeaky in the center of the stuffing in five minutes or less. I still buy the occasional stuffed toy, but I only give it to a dog when I have the time to sit and enjoy watching him tear it apart. I also like to be there to remove the toy's torn off legs or ears and make sure that the dog doesn't swallow wads of stuffing. I have also had Corgis who would bite out the noisemaker in squeaky toys or chew them to shreds. My girl Rhiannon adores squeaky toys. She likes to poke them with her nose or bite them, but she doesn't chew. So supervise and make sure that your Corgi's playtime is safe.

Toys don't have to be expensive either.

Toys don't have to be expensive—a carrot can be a wonderful chew toy for a young dog.

A carrot can be a wonderful chew toy for a young dog. My puppies have always enjoyed an open paper bag, and an empty plastic milk or juice carton is another free toy. The cardboard tubes from paper towel rolls and toilet paper can also supply some fun, and there's no harm done if your dog swallows a bit. Watch to see just how your puppy deals with this cardboard. If it looks like he's going to swallow large pieces, find another toy. If your puppy is teething, wet and then freeze an old washcloth for him to chew. The cold will soothe inflamed gums. Remember to remove the cloth before the puppy chews and swallows any of it.

Chapter
4

Feeding Your
Pembroke Welsh Corgi

Corgis are notorious chowhounds and will generally eat anything and everything. It's up to you to make sure that your dog eats a balanced diet and not a lot of empty calories. All dogs need the basic ingredients of good nutrition, and there are many ways to get those basics. Not every method is right for every dog, even within the same breed. Study your options, and decide which is best for your dog and which method you are most comfortable with. But keep in

Fat in the diet contributes to a healthy skin and coat.

mind that Corgis as a breed are not fussy eaters. They will eat just about anything they are offered.

The Building Blocks of Nutrition

All dogs need carbohydrates, fat, protein, vitamins, minerals, and water in the correct proportions to keep them healthy. Keep in mind that dogs need higher amounts of both protein and fat than people do, which is why a steady diet of "people food" may not be the best for your dog. If you plan to cook for your dog, or to feed a raw diet, keep in mind that a balanced diet for you is not the same as a balanced diet for your dog. Talk to a veterinary nutritionist so that you can offer your Corgi food that properly meets his dietary needs.

Carbohydrates

Carbohydrates supply energy and help with digestion. Grain fillers in dog food usually supply complex carbohydrates. In the wild, canines get their vegetables from the stomachs and intestines of the herbivores they eat. Carbohydrates provide slow, steady energy.

Fat

Fat supplies energy, as well as stores energy for future use and contributes to a healthy skin and coat. Fat also carries certain vitamins and helps the dog to use those vitamins. Fat adds flavor, and many

Puppy Love

HOW TO FEED YOUR NEW PUPPY

When you first bring your puppy home, feed him whatever the breeder was feeding him. Stick with that food for the first week or so. Then, if you want to change foods, go ahead. Just remember to take three or four days to make the change so that your puppy adjusts to the new food.

Puppies grow rapidly and need more calories than an adult dog. They also have smaller stomachs, and so your puppy will need three or four meals daily to make sure that he gets the nutrients he needs to grow. A puppy food is not necessary. Choose a good-quality adult food, and feed that. If you choose a dry food, select one with very small kibble. The package will say "mini chunks" or "small size" or something similar. The smaller kibble will be easier for your puppy to eat and digest. By the time he arrives at your house, he will probably be old enough to eat just three meals a day. At six months of age, reduce the meals to twice a day. At one year, you can feed just once a day, or you can continue with the twice-daily feeding. Corgis enjoy food so much that I've always given mine the opportunity to enjoy it twice a day. Just remember that twice a day doesn't mean twice as much. Divide the amount of food your dog eats in a day into two meals.

dry foods are sprayed with fat to tempt dogs to eat.

Protein

Protein is essential for growth and strong muscles, as well as for building a healthy coat and strong nails. Protein is made up of amino acids, and some proteins not in a dog's food can be produced in his body if he gets proper nutrition. Both lean meat and eggs (make sure that you cook them first) contain all of the essential amino acids that dogs need for good health. Look for meat, fish, eggs, and dairy on your dog food label.

Vitamins and Minerals

Vitamins and minerals help dogs process protein, fat, and carbohydrates, as well as help with bone growth and vision. They also help regulate growth and affect the nervous system. Minerals are crucial to healthy blood flow and healing.

Water

Water is another important nutrient. It makes up between 60 and 70 percent of the body weight of a dog and helps regulate body temperature, as well as carry other nutrients and oxygen throughout the body.

Dog Food Labels

When choosing a commercial food for your Corgi, start by reading the label. The first thing you'll find is that the food is approved by the AAFCO. AAFCO is the American Association of Feed Control Officials, the governing body for all animal feed products. It sets the guidelines for pet food manufacturers to ensure that the food is suitable for your pet. For instance, under AAFCO regulations, by-products may not include hair, horn, teeth, hooves, feathers, or manure. Regulations also require that all ingredients must be listed in order, from the largest amount to the smallest.

The first five ingredients are the most important. Somewhere in those five, preferably in first place, should be a meat protein. This is generally beef, chicken, turkey, or lamb, although more and more dog foods are based on fish. Meat by-

When choosing a commercial food for your Corgi, start by reading the label to make sure that he's receiving the nutrition he requires.

PUPPY FOOD

—Lucy Jones is a veterinarian and bred her first litter of Llanelly Corgis in 1978. Her grandmother was an obedience judge who started with English Cockers and later switched to Corgis. Lucy received her first Corgi from her grandmother when she was 15. She breeds for herself and wants sensible, healthy dogs who are fun to be around. She likes to put both a conformation championship and a Utility Dog title on the dogs she keeps. Her daughter, Olivia, is following in her footsteps.

Q: As a veterinarian and a breeder, do you recommend a puppy food, and if so, for how long?

A: I like to feed a high-protein puppy food until the puppy is 12 weeks old, and then I switch to an adult food. I add lots of calcium in the form of cottage cheese and milk because I feel that this helps with leg growth. It's important that a working dog have good legs and for Corgis to have a good front. I prefer adding the calcium this way rather than using supplements. I've had very good luck with giving all of my dogs dairy protein and less meat.

It's important to watch a Corgi's weight, and that is best done with a high-quality diet and exercise. They do better with a bit higher protein percentage and higher fat content, and with a high-quality food, they get what they need from a smaller amount.

products may also be listed in the first five ingredients. "By-products" may not sound too appetizing to us, but your dog will love them. By-products include organ meat, and they're full of vitamins and minerals for your dog.

Next on the label will likely be a grain filler. Manufacturers use grain to add bulk to the food. A grain filler is fine as long as there's more meat than filler in the food. Filler grains are corn, wheat, rice, and soy. You'll find corn in most dog foods because it's cheap. Next come wheat and soy. All three of these may cause allergies, so pay attention to how your dog reacts to his food. If he's scratching,or biting and chewing at his paws, he may be allergic to something in his food. Rice causes fewer allergic reactions and has become a popular filler for that reason.

Vitamins and minerals are frequently added to dog food to make it a complete and balanced diet for your dog. Preservatives may also be listed on the label. Preservatives are added to the food to give it a longer shelf life and to keep the food from spoiling. Vitamin E is a natural preservative, and you may

Commercial diets help owners maintain a proper nutritional balance for their dogs.

prefer that to a chemically produced preservative, but remember, natural preservatives don't last as long as chemical preservatives. They break down when exposed to light and air. If your food choice uses natural preservatives, buy the food in smaller quantities and store it in a cool, dark place, preferably in an airtight container.

Another thing to remember if you are trying to avoid preservatives is that manufacturers don't have to list a preservative if they don't add one, but there still may be preservatives in the bulk food they buy to produce their own branded product.

Your food label will also include a "guaranteed analysis," which tells you the percentage of each component. Look for a higher protein percentage if your dog is very active, a lower percentage if he is less active. For an overweight dog, look for a lower fat content.

Remember that the AAFCO does not regulate quality. You still need to make the decision as to whether or not you feel the ingredients are what your dog needs to stay healthy.

Commercial Diets

Maintaining a proper nutritional balance is why many people rely on commercial dog food, but even with this type of diet, not every kind is good for every dog. You may get a recommendation from a friend for the brand of food she feeds her dog, and her dog may do very well on the food, but your dog might not. Just as individual people have food allergies and reactions to particular foods, so do dogs.

Many people, especially after the pet food recalls, want to use a commercial food without artificial preservatives or without grain. Fortunately, more and more commercial foods offer these options. There are also foods that are made entirely with human-grade ingredients and some that are entirely organic. There is even a vegetarian food on the market, although there is some discussion as to whether dogs can thrive without meat protein in their diet.

If you choose a commercial food, whether you decide to go with dry, canned, or semi-moist, read the label first so that you know just what your Corgi is going to get.

Dry Food (Kibble)

Dry foods are the most economical and don't need to be refrigerated. They are convenient and offer your dog something to chew, although most Corgis I know tend to gulp their food without much chewing. Most brand-name foods of any type will provide a good balanced diet, with little variation between one batch and the next, and will have fewer fillers. Generally, dry foods have more filler than canned foods. If you choose a commercial dry food, you can add cooked or raw meat, cooked eggs, cottage cheese, and lightly cooked vegetables once or twice a week if you'd like.

Canned Food

Canned food is frequently more expensive than dry food and needs to be refrigerated after the can is opened. Most dogs love canned food because it smells good (to them, at least) and also tastes good. If you decide on a canned food, make sure that your dog isn't just getting filler and water. Usually, canned foods have a higher protein content than dry foods. Remember, too, that because canned food has more water, you'll need to feed proportionally more. A Corgi eating a cup of dry food a day will need between a can and a can and a half of the canned food.

Semi-Moist Food

Semi-moist foods are your third choice if you are selecting a commercial diet. These foods come in a pouch or other kind of packet and are frequently shaped like ground meat, a burger, or chicken. These foods are soft and are also more likely to contain cornstarch, or flour, as well as sugar, to help keep them soft. There is likely to be more food coloring and more preservatives in these types of food as well. If price is a consideration, semi-moist foods are frequently more expensive than either dry or canned foods.

Non-Commercial Diets

If you want to avoid commercial foods altogether, your options are to cook for your Corgi, using human-grade ingredients, or feed a raw diet.

Raw Diet

The raw diet is frequently called the BARF diet. Those letters stand for either "Bones and Raw Food," or "Biologically Appropriate Raw Food." If you decide to follow the BARF diet, you'll be feeding both muscle meat and organ meat, as well as prepared fruits and vegetables. Grains are optional. For instance, you may feed your Corgi three raw chicken wings

DRY AND CANNED FOOD COMPARISON

The website www.bigpawsonly.com offers a formula for determining just how much protein, fat, and fiber is in a food. Using this formula, you can compare dry and canned foods to determine just what nutrition your dog is getting. Remove the moisture content so that you have a dry-weight percentage. Dry kibble has a moisture content of about 10 percent, while canned food has a moisture content of 75 percent. Find the percentage of protein, fat, or fiber, and the moisture percentage. Subtract the moisture percentage from 100, and then divide the protein, fat, or fiber percentage by that number. Multiply by 100 and that gives you your dry-weight percentage.

in one meal and a mixture of vegetables in the next. Raw meat can be poultry, beef, venison, rabbit, lamb, or whatever you prefer. Fish is also good, but many advocates of raw feeding suggest cooking fish first to kill parasites that may be in the meat. Vegetables will need to be broken down in a blender, as dogs can't digest the cellulose of plant cell walls, and processing helps break up the cellulose. Freezing the blended mixture further helps break down the cellulose. If you decide to add grains to the diet, they must either be soaked for about 12 hours, or you need to cook them.

There doesn't seem to be a middle ground when people talk about the BARF diet. Many feel that the risk of bacterial infection is too great, while others contend that the canine digestive tract is meant to handle this type of food and that the benefits of raw food, with no preservatives or processing, outweigh the risks. If you decide to feed raw food to your Corgi, consider freezing the food first to help kill some of the bacteria. Just make sure that you thaw it before you give it to your Corgi, as frozen bones can be as deadly as cooked bones, which can splinter, and if swallowed, can cause damage to the intestines.

A raw diet is not as convenient as feeding commercial foods because you need freezer room for the food, and if you are traveling or are boarding your dog, you need to make provisions to carry the food with you or to make sure that the boarding facility can handle this type of food. If you're on the road with your dog, you may not be able to easily restock, although more and more pet supply stores offer frozen raw food. This makes it easier to consider this type of diet because the food is prepackaged, and you don't need to find a source for your raw bones or your chicken necks.

The raw food diet doesn't mean that you just give your dog bones and raw meat at random. There is a definite ratio of bones to meat and grains. You may also want to supplement with vitamins. Also, if you want to start your puppy on a raw diet, you may want to grind the bones, as young dogs cannot always properly chew up large bones. If

If you decide to feed raw food to your Corgi, consider freezing it first to help kill some of the bacteria.

A balanced diet is critical to your Corgi's good health and well-being.

you decide to feed your Corgi raw food, consult with your vet. If you've found the perfect veterinarian but she is not happy about your decision to feed raw, have a basic blood test and repeat every six months so that your veterinarian can see that all blood levels are as they should be. It's your choice as to how you feed your dog, but you don't want to lose a good vet in an argument over feeding.

Home-Cooked Diet

If you want to avoid commercial foods but are a bit skittish about raw feeding, you can cook for your Corgi. This offers the safety of thoroughly cooked foods and the quality of human-grade food without the dangers of bacteria in raw foods or the preservatives and high processing of commercial foods. As with a raw diet, you will probably need some freezer space so that you can cook up large batches of the food at one time, although I do know an owner who feels that it's quick and easy to throw all of the ingredients into a pot each morning, cook for half an hour, cool, and serve. Traveling and boarding considerations are the same with cooked food as with the raw diet. Consult with your veterinarian about what possible vitamin and mineral supplements you may need to make your home-cooked food a balanced diet for your Corgi.

Feeding Schedule

Many people like to "free-feed" their dog. This means filling a bowl with the daily allotment and putting it down for the dog to munch on throughout the day. It's hard to imagine this working with a Corgi, as most will eat whatever is in front of them instantly. Also, if you have more than one dog, the pushier dog may get his food, plus his pal's as well. Free-feeding only works with dry food. It's not a good idea to leave canned food out all day, and semi-moist foods will dry out. You must never leave out home-cooked or raw foods. The risk of harmful bacteria growth is too great. Scheduled feeding is a much better option. With scheduled feeding, you set the food bowl down for an allotted amount of time and then pick it up again until the next meal.

Corgis may be fed once a day, but I like breaking up the food into two meals. This also helps if the dogs need medication with their food, as it gives you two set times to sneak the medicine into their food.

Obesity

No matter how or what you feed your Corgi, keep an eye on his waistline. Corgis tend to eat anything and everything, and

INTRODUCING NEW FOODS

The accepted wisdom used to be that once you had settled on a particular food for your dog, you never changed it. If you did change, the change was done gradually, over a period of four or five days. Many people now feel that it's better to feed a variety. Some people change what they feed every day. Others rotate between three or four types of commercial food, or they mix a couple together. This feeding plan means that your dog's intestinal tract can better cope with anything new, and your dog is less apt to become ill from eating a strange food.

they are experts at the art of begging. Limit extra treats, or factor them into the amount of food given daily. Make sure that your Corgi gets plenty of exercise. If you notice him getting a bit plump, cut back on the food and see if you can increase his exercise. Seen from above, your Corgi should show an indentation behind the ribs. You should be able to feel your dog's ribs under his coat. You shouldn't be able to see the ribs; that means the other extreme, and your dog will need more food.

Forbidden Foods

Some foods are on the forbidden list no matter how you choose to feed your dog. Chocolate heads the list. Chocolate contains theobromine, and the darker the chocolate, the more theobromine it contains. Your Corgi might be fine after stealing a bite of your candy bar, but just three ounces of baking chocolate could be fatal. Xylitol is an artificial sweetener that is toxic to dogs. It's commonly used to sweeten gum, but you can also purchase it to use in cooking. Check the labels of

No matter how or what you feed your Corgi, keep an eye on his waistline.

Check It Out

FEEDING CHECKLIST

✓ Read the labels on dog food to help make the right choice for your dog.

✓ If buying dry food, buy in the smallest quantity possible to help keep it fresh.

✓ Store dry food in an airtight container. Keep open cans in the refrigerator. Also, refrigerate any raw or fresh ingredients.

✓ Look for signs of an allergic reaction. Even a premium dog food can contain something that affects your particular dog.

✓ Watch your Corgi's weight and limit treats.

✓ Always supply plenty of clean drinking water.

✓ Wash food and water dishes daily.

any artificially sweetened products, and keep them out of reach of your Corgi.

Other foods to be careful of are grapes, raisins, onions, and egg whites. You don't need to panic if your dog eats a couple of raisins or a grape, but if he finds an entire box of raisins and thinks it is a wonderful snack, check in with your veterinarian. Onions can cause hemolytic anemia, and raw egg whites (cooked are fine) contain a protein called avidin, which can deplete biotin, a B vitamin, in your dog. Again, don't panic if your dog eats some raw egg white, but don't make raw egg whites a regular part of your dog's diet.

Too many macadamia nuts can

cause temporary paralysis of the hindquarters. The paralysis will wear off, but it's frightening when it happens, and sometimes the paralysis is misdiagnosed: People have been known to have their dog euthanized, thinking he was permanently paralyzed.

Coffee and tea may perk you up, but both of these beverages contain caffeine and theobromine, so they're on your dog's "can't have" list as well.

Also, avoid all cooked bones, which can splinter and cause intestinal damage. Remember that after a day or two, raw bones can dry out and be as dangerous as cooked bones.

Chapter
5

Grooming Your
Pembroke Welsh Corgi

orgis are frequently called a "wash-and-wear" breed because they don't need much grooming, but all dogs need some kind of grooming care, and Corgis are no exception. That lovely double coat, which protects your Corgi from all kinds of weather, needs to be brushed regularly to remove loose, dead hair; nails need to be trimmed; teeth should be brushed; and ears should be inspected.

Grooming Tools

You won't need many grooming tools; these are some you might want to consider:

- **Comb(s).** Dog combs are made of metal and come with varying numbers of teeth per inch (cm). A medium comb will work well for combing out your Corgi. You may also want a flea comb. Flea combs have very closely spaced teeth for trapping fleas. A Greyhound comb has wider-spaced

You will need a metal dog comb to groom your Corgi.

Puppy Love

PUGGY GROOMING

Puppies don't need much grooming except for their nails. As long as their ears and eyes are clear, puppies, unless they get into a mud puddle, don't need baths or brushing. However, puppyhood is a good time to get your Corgi used to grooming, especially nail trimming. Hold each of your puppy's feet for a few seconds every day. Be gentle, and give the feet a little massage. Work at taking just the tip of the nail off with your nail clippers. Don't worry so much about really shortening the nails as about getting your puppy used to the process. If you've decided on a grinder, turn it on and hold a paw against the body of the grinder so that your Corgi can feel the vibration and get used to the noise. Run a soft bristle brush over your Corgi's back and sides to get him used to the feel of a brush. Again, the goal isn't to remove any fur but just to let him know that nothing is going to hurt him.

teeth for half the length and closer-set teeth for the other half.

- **Ear cleaner (optional).** Special ear cleaners make it easy to clean out wax and dirt, but unless your Corgi has a real problem, you can achieve the same effect with a damp cloth or cotton balls.
- **Grooming table (optional).** A grooming table is a folding table with a rubber mat top. It's useful because it brings the dog up to your level. It's a must if you will be showing your Corgi.
- **Hair dryer (optional).** Dog hair dryers are cooler than the human equivalent. As long as your dog is in a warm, dry place, he can air-dry after a bath.
- **Nail clippers.** Nail clippers come in several styles and are used to keep your dog's nails short. They all do the job,

but some people prefer one type over another. Talk to your breeder or other dog owners about their preferences.

- **Nail grinders.** Dremel grinders are electric or battery-powered tools with a rapidly rotating abrasive head at one end. It is this abrasive head that wears down the nails. Many Corgis prefer having their nails ground rather than cut.
- **Slicker brush.** This brush has thin wire bristles with a slight bend at the top.
- **Small spray bottle.** This is useful for lightly dampening the coat before brushing.
- **Soft bristle brush (optional).** A soft brush gives a nice finished look to your dog's coat. It's good to have if you're showing your dog.
- **Tiny baby brush (optional).** A small, soft brush suitable for a human baby,

Brushing your Corgi on a regular basis will help keep down the amount of fur that drifts through your house.

• **Towels.** You'll need lots of towels. Save your old bath towels when you replace them. Yard sales or thrift stores may also be a good source for old towels.

Brushing

Brushing a Corgi is not hard, and if you do it on a regular basis, it will help keep down the amount of Corgi fur that drifts through your house. Corgis have a double coat, with a thick, soft undercoat and a harsher outercoat. It's the undercoat that needs to be combed out.

How to Brush

Start by putting your Corgi up on a sturdy, nonslip surface. You can brush your dog at floor level, but that makes it easier for him to get away from you, and it's harder on your back. If you have a grooming table, great. Otherwise, cover your bed with a sheet or towel and use that. Or buy a small rubber-backed rug and use the top of your clothes dryer. Outdoors, a picnic table is a good height.

Lightly spray the coat with water to prevent it from breaking and to help keep it from flying all over. If you like, add a small amount of Listerine to the water. It helps clean the coat and leaves it smelling fresh. Start at the back of your dog, and with one hand, push the coat against the grain. Using your slicker brush, work from the skin out, brushing the undercoat. Work your way forward, patch by patch.

this brush works well if you are using powder, chalk, or cornstarch to whiten your Corgi's feet before going into the conformation show ring.
• **Toothbrush and paste.** Some doggy toothbrushes are made to fit over your index finger and have rubber bristles at the tip. Others look like a human toothbrush. Dog toothpaste comes in flavors dogs like, usually beef or chicken.

Another technique is to just start brushing against the grain. Your slicker brush will snag out all the loose undercoat. Combing with the grain will straighten things out and will also remove loose hair. Depending on how much coat your Corgi has, weekly combing may be all that's needed. My male has a very thick undercoat. When I brush him, I could build another Corgi with the hair that comes out. My female has much less coat. Combing alone works well to keep her looking neat and tidy.

Be gentle when using the slicker brush. Take into consideration how much fur your Corgi has so that you aren't scratching his skin. Don't use the slicker on the lower legs or on the face or ears. Whether you're using the brush or a comb, if you hit a snag, stop. Use your fingers to gently work out any tangles,

then resume combing. The same applies to the longer hair on the back of your Corgi's rear legs. Hold your hand at the base of the fur and comb from the base up to prevent harsh tugging and pulling.

Bathing

Your Corgi is not going to need a lot of baths if you keep up with your brushing routine. A good bath will loosen up dead hair and get you through a major shed a bit faster, and if you show your dog in conformation, you'll probably bathe him more often. Rain and snow help keep the outercoat clean. If you live in the Southwest, where it's hot, dry, and dusty, your Corgi may need a bath more often. If you have an infestation of fleas, a bath is definitely in order, but otherwise, once or twice a year is more than enough. If you feel better giving your Corgi a bath every

GROOMING AS A HEALTH CHECK

Although a good brushing once a week is ideal, your Corgi's coat won't mat or snarl like some breeds, so if you skip a week, it's not a horrible crime. Still, try to groom your dog at least once a month. Nails, especially, need attention, but there's another reason for regular grooming. Grooming allows you to check your dog all over for any lumps, bumps, or bug bites. Inspecting the ears gives you a chance to notice any wax buildup or discharge. When you trim foot fur and nails, inspect the footpads for any abrasions or cracks. Pushing back the fur for brushing and running your hands over your dog's body will help you discover any odd growths. Grooming is also a good time to inspect for fleas and ticks as well.

three or four months, go ahead.

No matter what bath schedule you follow, there is a method to doing a good job. If you have a stationary tub in your basement, your Corgi might fit, and that will save your back. If you have multiple dogs, having a tub installed at the right height may be a good investment. Otherwise, you'll need to use the tub in your bathroom. You can invest in a special faucet attachment that supplies a spray head for wetting your dog. There are

Your Corgi will rarely need to be bathed.

also shower attachments, and these work very well when washing a dog. Another alternative is to use a saucepan or an unbreakable pitcher to pour the water over your dog.

How to Bathe

The first step is to get all of your supplies together. You don't want to have a soggy Corgi in the tub and then realize that the shampoo is downstairs. Get a rubber mat for the tub bottom so that your dog has secure footing. Get lots of towels. Get another one. Get your dog shampoo. Always use a dog shampoo on your dog because it has the correct pH for canines. Human shampoo can dry your dog's coat and may make his skin dry and itchy as well. If you want to use a coat conditioner, get that as well. I like to add vinegar to the final rinse. This helps get rid of soap residue and adds some shine to the coat. If you're going to put cotton in your dog's ears, get that. Have a soft cloth handy for washing off the face and ears. Get something to kneel on. A rubber pad is ideal, or cover a pillow with towels. (It will get wet, so a feather pillow is not a good idea.) Whatever you are wearing while you bathe your Corgi will get wet, so consider that and change clothes if necessary. You may also want to keep a collar on your dog while he's in the tub to help you keep him in one spot. A collar also makes it easier to grab a soapy Corgi who may try to escape.

Once you have all of the supplies, go get your dog and lead him to the bathroom. Give him a treat or two to keep him happy. Shut the door. Trust me, you don't want a wet, soapy Corgi running through the house. If you want to put cotton in your dog's ears, now is the time. It's been my experience that a Corgi will shake his head until the cotton is dislodged, so I don't use cotton. I am careful with the spray, and if I need to rinse soap from the dog's neck, I fold the ear over or rinse away the soap with a wet cloth.

Before you put your dog in the tub, get the water to the correct temperature. Lukewarm is good. Test it on the inside of your wrist. If you're comfortable, your dog will be too. Now add the dog to the mix and thoroughly wet his coat all the way to the skin. Just spraying or pouring over the top won't do it; you have to work the water through the coat. If you want to wipe off your dog's face with a damp cloth, this is a good time. Don't use soap; just warm water will be enough.

Now add shampoo. If you suspect fleas, start at the neck and make a collar of suds, then work backward so that the fleas are chased away from your dog's head. Rinse and suds up again. Make sure that you wash your dog's stomach, his feet, and where each leg joins the body. Rinse. Rinse again. Rinse one more time. Make sure that all of the soap is out of the coat, and pay special attention to the

Ask the Expert

GROOMING FREQUENCY

—Julia Clough, Corgi breeder

Q: How often do you recommend brushing and bathing a Corgi, as well as trimming his nails?

A: I recommend a weekly combing. Spray the coat lightly with water and comb out any dead hair. The water prevents the coat from breaking and also helps keep the hair from flying around. A bath can be a good idea when your Corgi is blowing his coat twice a year, as a warm bath will help loosen the coat and hurry the shedding process. Otherwise, Corgis are clean dogs, and the weekly combing should be enough. Of course, this also depends on the individual dog. I use a grinder on my dogs' nails to try to grind them every two weeks. Once a month may be enough, depending on how fast an individual dog's nails grow. Regular walks on pavement can help keep the nails worn down.

stomach and where each leg is attached. Add about half a cup of vinegar to your final rinse if you want to.

Once your dog is rinsed, hold him in the tub a minute or two. With luck, he will shake once or twice. It's amazing how much water will come out of his coat that way. Next, wrap a towel around him and lift him from the tub. Don't let him scramble out by himself, as he could get hurt. Towel dry. Use two or three towels. As you're drying him, he'll probably shake

Your Corgi's nails will probably need to be trimmed at least once a month.

a few more times. Keep the room door shut until he's finished and that's it. In cool weather, keep your dog indoors until he is dry. In nice weather, you can let him out, but don't be surprised if the first thing he does is roll. Just hope that he rolls in clean grass and not in the nearest pile of dirt!

Air-drying is fine, but if you are going to be giving multiple dogs baths year round, a canine hair dryer might be a good investment. At one time, one of my Corgis had a skin infection that required a daily bath. I bought a hair dryer to hasten the drying process. It is possible to use a hair dryer for humans, but if that's your choice, use the air-only setting. Most dryers made for humans are much too hot for a dog's skin.

Nail Care

Nails grow at different rates but will probably need to be trimmed at least once a month. If you walk your Corgi on a sidewalk regularly, however, you might not ever need to trim.

Nails that are too long make it hard for your dog to walk, and they also tend to pull the toes away from each other, giving your dog a splayed foot that is unattractive and can interfere with his movement. Long nails can also catch and break, which can be painful and may get infected.

How to Care for the Nails

When you cut the nails, avoid the quick, which is the dark blood vessel running through the middle of the nail. If your Corgi has black nails, you won't be able to see the quick. Cut the nail just where it curves, and you should be safe. If you accidentally cut the quick, use a touch of styptic powder to stop the bleeding or just hold your finger tightly to the end of the nail until the bleeding stops.

If you're grinding your Corgi's nails, don't just hold the wheel against the nail. Move it around the nail, and stop at intervals to let heat dissipate.

Ear Care

Corgis, with their nice, upright ears, don't generally have many ear problems. The ears' upright position enables the air to reach the inner ear, so there's no dark, moist area for infections. That's not to say that your Corgi can't have a problem, but daily ear care is not necessary.

How to Care for the Ears

When you're brushing your Corgi or when he's beside you on the couch while you're watching television, take a look at his ears. The inner surface should be clean, and the surfaces you can see should be pink. If the ear is red or inflamed, or there's a discharge or lots of dirt, it's time to act. For surface dirt, squirt some ear cleaner on a cotton ball or use warm water. Swab out the ear, but don't poke or push. Don't try to reach beyond the area you can see.

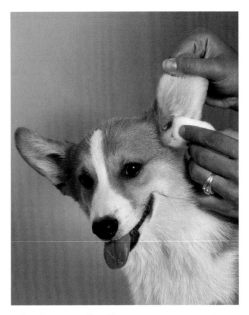

To clean your Corgi's ears, never use a cotton swab—use a cotton ball or soft wipe instead.

If your Corgi is scratching at his ear, shaking his head frequently, or holding his head to the side, he may have an infection. Corgis can get ear mites, as well as yeast infections, or dirt can get into the ear. Take your Corgi to your veterinarian for proper diagnosis and treatment.

Eye Care

Fortunately, there's not much you need to worry about with a Corgi's eyes. Corgis don't get tearstains, so there's no grooming issue there, and unlike some breeds, whose eyes tend to protrude a bit, putting them more at risk for injuries, a

Corgi's eyes are well set in his face. Corgis can accidentally injure an eye, but it's not common.

How to Care for the Eyes

If you notice that your dog's eye is weepy or swollen, or if he is squinting, keeping one eye closed, or pawing at an eye, seek medical attention. Occasionally, you may notice a bit of matter in the corner, but just dampen a facial tissue and wipe it

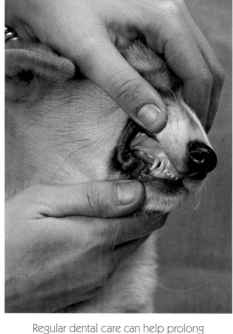

Regular dental care can help prolong your dog's life because he will not suffer from periodontal disease.

away. There's no need to worry unless this is a chronic condition.

Dental Care

Dental care is easily overlooked, but statistics show that 75 percent of all dogs have some kind of periodontal problem by the time they are four years old. So include your Corgi's mouth and teeth as part of your grooming routine.

Dental care is as important in dogs as it is in people, and starting young will help protect your dog's health. Although dogs are not as susceptible to tooth decay as humans, they do develop plaque, which if not removed, hardens to tartar. Tartar, in turn, can cause abscesses, and the bacteria from those abscesses can circulate in the dog's system and lead to pneumonia or heart, liver, or kidney problems.

How to Care for the Teeth

Start tooth care gradually with your puppy. Wrap a bit of gauze around your finger and gently rub it over his teeth and gums. You may want to flavor the gauze by rubbing a bit of hot dog or cheese over it. Praise your puppy and reward with a treat after each session. After a week or so of this, graduate to a canine toothbrush. You may choose one that is similar to a human toothbrush, or you may prefer the rubber ones that fit on your index finger and have rubber bristles.

Check It Out

GROOMING CHECKLIST

✓ Brush and comb your Corgi once a week.

✓ Brush your dog's teeth at least once a week. Three times a week is better. Every day is wonderful.

✓ Clip nails every two weeks.

✓ Check ears when you clip nails. Ears should be clean, odorless, and pink.

✓ Eyes don't need a specific check, but if an eye doesn't look normal or your dog is squinting or pawing at an eye, see your veterinarian.

✓ Bathe once or twice a year.

Flavored doggy toothpaste will increase your dog's willingness to let you brush his teeth. Never use human toothpaste on your dog. Dogs don't rinse and spit, and too much swallowed human toothpaste can make your dog ill. Brush daily if you can, or at least weekly, to help keep your dog's mouth and teeth healthy.

There may come a time when your veterinarian recommends a professional cleaning for your dog's teeth. This entails anesthetizing your dog. The veterinarian or technician then removes any tartar buildup and cleans and polishes your dog's teeth, much like your dentist cleans your own teeth. If any cracked or broken teeth are found, they'll remove those. If there are any abscesses or if there is infection anywhere in the gum, your dog will probably be put on an antibiotic. If your dog is older, the veterinarian may also recommend blood tests before the cleaning to make sure that the dog can safely handle the anesthesia. This safeguard is well worth it, and with older dogs, may help your veterinarian detect other health problems as well.

Not all dogs are alike, of course. Some dogs may need their teeth cleaned every six months; some may go their entire lives without needing a professional cleaning. Have your veterinarian check your dog's teeth at least once a year, and if you notice that your Corgi's breath smells more than his normal "dog breath" or if he is drooling, pawing at his mouth, or having trouble eating hard food and no longer wants to chew on toys or bones, make an appointment with your veterinarian.

Chapter 6

Training Your Pembroke Welsh Corgi

There's a saying that an untrained dog is an unhappy dog. I don't know how true that is, but I do know that people around an untrained dog are frequently unhappy and that lack of training is a leading cause of dogs being turned into animal shelters. Even if you don't care if your dog has no manners, chances are that friends and family will care. Jumping, barking, begging dogs are no fun to be around, and even a dog the size of a Corgi can knock someone over, leading to a possible injury. Another reason to train your dog is that it is a good way to bond with him, as well as giving him something to think about. Corgis need a job, and learning can be that job.

Positive Training

There are many different ways to train your puppy, but training theories have come a long way from the old methods of training collars and sharp corrections. Today, a positive approach is recommended. Behavior consultant Ken McCort says that people punish dogs because they can, not because it's necessary or advisable. After all, no one puts a training collar on a killer whale or a dolphin, yet both of these animals can be successfully trained. Positive training rewards good behavior, but it also works at redirecting a dog's energy. Instead of scolding or punishing a dog for jumping,

A trained dog will make your life easier even when just grooming him.

for instance, a positive trainer gives no attention to a jumping dog and instead rewards the dog the minute he stops jumping.

Clicker training is a well-known method of positive training. The clicker, which is a small noisemaker, marks precisely the action that you want your dog to perform. A treat follows. The clicker noise lets your dog know immediately that he has done something of which you approve and that you will soon be rewarding him.

Some people find it too much to handle a dog lead, treats, and a clicker, and it does take some learning on the handler's part, but it's a very effective way to train. The clicker is a neutral sound, with no emotional overtones. If you just can't manage the clicker, you can substitute a marker word that means the same thing—it marks the action just like the clicker. You can use any word, but it's a good idea not to use one that you will be using at any other time. For instance, I say "Good dog" quite often, so "good" is not a word I should use as a marker in training. Corgis are smart enough to figure out the difference, but why complicate things?

Another reason that punishment doesn't work well is that many things dogs do make them feel good. The punishment may stop them briefly, but the action they were engaged in releases chemicals in the brain and feels so good that it overrides any fear of punishment.

Socialization

Socialization is a form of training. It means exposing your Corgi to as many new experiences as possible in a positive way so that he approaches life with curiosity and confidence instead of being shy and fearful. If a new event means praise and a treat, your Corgi will approach anything new with an upbeat attitude. As early as possible, expose your Corgi to new sights and sounds, as well as to different people, and especially children. Besides having high voices and often jerky movements, children are likely to want to pet your Corgi, often without asking permission. They may even hug or try to pick up your dog, and believe me, a child can have your dog in her arms before you can move to stop her. It's good to have a dog who's used to other dogs and possibly cats, but it's essential that your dog be accustomed to children. Do remember that introductions need to be controlled. Letting your puppy out with several children who are running and playing may trigger the dog's herding instinct, which is to chase what's running and nip it on the ankle. That can mean frightened children and a puppy who thinks that this is acceptable behavior.

How to Socialize

Start socializing as soon as you get your puppy. In fact, your breeder will have started the process with the normal coming and going of people in the house, radio and television programs playing, and the rattle of pots and pans.

Continue to let your puppy be part of the

Your dog should be socialized to other pets and people, especially children.

household with all of its different noises. Let your puppy experience different textures underfoot, like carpeting, linoleum, pavement, grass, and gravel. Put down an old screen and walk your puppy over the metal. Some people set up small obstacle courses for their puppies, with tunnels, some shallow steps, a small bridge, and a metal grate to walk over. Leave an open umbrella lying around or another odd object. Just remember to supervise play. You don't want your puppy to become frightened or injured. When you bring a new item into your home, let your puppy smell it. Give a command, like "sniff," or "smell it," and when he does, praise and treat. Go where there are lots of different people. Carry your puppy into the bank, or walk around outside a shopping mall. (Most malls won't let you go indoors). Carry lots of treats, and let willing strangers pet your puppy and give him a treat. If you don't have children, offer to do a program for a Scout troop or a youth group. You can teach children the proper way to approach and pet a dog, and at the same time, you are introducing your puppy to a dozen or more children.

A puppy kindergarten class can help your puppy get used to both people and other dogs in a positive setting, or maybe you can arrange a play date in a fenced yard for your puppy and friendly neighborhood dogs. Try to arrange play dates with dogs who are close to the size of your Corgi. A large dog may be friendly, but sheer size may mean that the dog is overwhelming, and he may even injure your dog accidentally while playing.

Crate Training

A crate is one of the most useful items you can own when you have a dog. Besides being a wonderful tool in housetraining, a dog who is used to a crate can be crated when you need him out of the way during a party or even during dinner preparation, and your dog will adjust better if there's an occasion when he needs to stay at the vet's. A teething puppy can wreak havoc on home furnishings, so for the first six months to a year of your puppy's life, crate him when you're away from home. He won't be able to hurt himself, and your chair legs will be safe from Corgi teeth. Crates also keep your dog safe while riding in the car, so start teaching your Corgi to use a crate right away. If he is a puppy, crate training will be easy. In fact, the breeder may have already started teaching your puppy about crates. A crate may seem expensive, but it will last the life of your dog, so get a good one.

How to Crate Train

Start crate training by leaving the door of the crate open. Feed your puppy in the crate with the door open. Periodically, throw a treat or a toy in the crate. Let the puppy come and go as he pleases. It won't take long for him to associate the crate with good things. The next day, put his food in the crate and close the door while he's eating. Open it the minute he finishes. Between meals, tempt him with a toy or a treat, and shut the door for a minute or two. If he's had a good play session and looks like he needs a nap, pop him in the crate for the nap. Most dogs take to the crate with no trouble at all and appreciate the privacy and security it gives them. By the end of a week, you should be able to put your puppy in his crate at any time, and he should sleep in his crate at night.

If you have an older dog, crate training may take a bit longer, but follow the same steps. Don't shut the door until your dog

Puppy Love

TRAINING A PUPPY

Puppies learn quickly, and there's no such thing as a puppy who's too young to train. Your local training classes may not accept young dogs until they have a complete set of shots, but that shouldn't stop you from beginning to train and socialize your puppy. Start teaching your puppy the basic commands the minute he settles into his new home. Just remember to keep all training positive. No yelling, no hitting, no jerking with the lead. In fact, you can begin your training with no collar or lead at all. If you don't want to work with a clicker, choose a word that lets your puppy know that he's done what you wanted. Use lots of treats, and keep your sessions short. Your Corgi can learn at a young age, but because he's a puppy, his powers of concentration won't be that of an adult. Several short sessions are better than one or two long ones.

is very comfortable with going in for food and treats. Be patient and don't rush it, and before you know it your dog will be going into the crate on his own for naps.

Housetraining

There are many different ways to housetrain your dog, but using the crate is one of the most efficient. Other methods may be better for a particular household, and these will also be discussed, but if you can use a crate to help housetrain, do so. Dogs don't like to eliminate where they sleep, so if confined to their crate, they will try not to eliminate. A crate offers a small, contained space, and if used properly, helps teach your puppy where to "go." There's work involved, of course. You can't just leave your puppy in a crate all day. That would defeat the purpose because there's only so long a puppy can "hold it" before he goes, bed or no bed.

How to Houstrain

Let's start with bedtime. If possible, have a crate in your bedroom. This will give your puppy some time with you with no effort on your part. Plus, if your puppy needs to go out in the middle of the night, you'll hear him whine and can get him outdoors. This will help reinforce the housetraining process.
Make sure

that the crate is in a draft-free area and that your puppy has a nice warm bed. If he gets cold in the night, he'll wake up, and if he wakes up, he'll have to go. Most Corgi puppies will start sleeping straight through the night very soon, but in the beginning, be prepared to make a few midnight excursions to the backyard. Keep your shoes or boots handy, as well as a coat if you're housetraining in cool weather. Pick up your puppy and take him outdoors. Don't set him down and expect him to follow you through the house, as he will go before you ever get outside. Snap a lead on his collar and take him to your designated spot. Praise him when he goes, give him a little treat if you're awake enough, and go back to bed.

When you get up in the morning, take your puppy out first thing, then pop him in his crate while you get your day started. Feed your puppy and take him out right after feeding. Bring him in and play with him a bit, then go back outside, then put him into his crate while you eat your own breakfast and finish the rest of your morning routine. Just before you leave for the day, take him outside one more time. If there's someone home all day, that will make housetraining that much faster, as whoever is at home can take the puppy out every couple of hours. If not, he should be fine for three or four hours in his crate, but he will need a noon break. If you can't get home, arrange for a neighbor or pet sitter to take care of your puppy. He'll need to go out, be fed, go out again, have some playtime, and then go back into his crate.

If there are children coming home from school, your puppy will be out again between three and four, and children also guarantee some playtime. The puppy should go out again at dinnertime, get fed, go out again, and get some playtime. Your puppy can be crated while you eat and then be taken out again. During the evening, your puppy may be eager to play, or he may just fall asleep while you're watching television. As long as someone is watching him, he can be out of his crate. Just make sure that he doesn't wander off on his own. An unsupervised puppy can get into all kinds of trouble, including chewing through an electric cord, with tragic results.

At bedtime, take your puppy outdoors one last time, give him a biscuit or a bit of dog food, as he will sleep better with something in his stomach, and then put him to bed.

Remember to always take your puppy to the same spot in the yard. The smell will help remind him of what you want him to do. Take him out on a lead so that he doesn't just scamper off to play. Sometimes puppies get so focused

A well-trained dog is a joy to have around.

on playing that they forget what they need to do until they are back inside. Remember, too, that dogs are creatures of habit. Follow a schedule, and your housetraining will go much faster. If you catch your puppy going indoors, don't holler at him—just pick him up and carry him to his spot in the yard. Praise him if he goes where he's supposed to. If your puppy goes indoors, it does no good to drag him to the spot and scold him. He's not going to know why you're yelling; it's too late. Just clean up the mess, making

If you follow a schedule, the housetraining process will go much faster.

sure that you don't use an ammonia-based cleaner. There's ammonia in urine, so a spot that smells like ammonia is a signal to your puppy that this is where he should go again.

Another point to remember is that, during the housetraining period, use the same door all the time. If one member of the family uses the back door and another uses the front door, it will take your puppy longer to connect going to a specific door when he wants to go out. Once he's fully trained, you can take him out any door, but chances are when he asks to go out, he'll always use the same door you used when you were training him.

It also helps to have a word or phrase that is associated with your puppy eliminating. I have always said, "Hurry up," but you can use anything. Besides helping to remind your puppy of why he is outside, it can be useful if it's pouring rain or you're rushing to go somewhere.

Puppies housetrain much faster than

humans, and soon you can trust your puppy to have the run of the house when someone is home.

Paper Training

Paper training is the practice of covering a floor with newspapers and gradually reducing the area until you finally pick up all the papers. In the meantime, when someone is with the dog, he is being taken outdoors to eliminate. This method works, but it may take a bit longer than when using a crate. Follow the same schedule as with using a crate. Confine your puppy to the area with the papers when you're not home. Take him outdoors after feeding, after naps, and after play sessions. Gradually reduce the area covered by paper until your puppy is asking to go out each time he needs to eliminate.

Other Methods

Sometimes apartment dwellers, especially those on upper floors, housetrain their dogs to a specific area in the apartment, rather than taking the dogs outside. I think that Corgis are a bit big for this, but if it works for you, that's all that matters. There are many different types of indoor dog toilet areas. Many have artificial turf and a post for male dogs. Liquids run through the surface cover and are caught in a tray, and solids are scooped. You can also use a large litter box, just like those used for cats. If you choose this method, remember to buy special dog litter.

You will train your Corgi to the litter box or to the special toilet area in the same way that you housetrain for outdoor elimination. After feeding, after naps, and after playtime, take the puppy to the appropriate location. Praise when he goes in the right place. Scoop solids but leave a bit of the wet litter, or leave a wet pad, so that the puppy can use his nose to return to the right place. Special housetraining

Housetraining is training your dog to potty outside.

Treats are an integral part of positive training.

yet what that something is. Don't be surprised if your dog runs through his entire repertoire of behaviors, trying to find the one you might want.

With or without a clicker, keep training sessions short, and don't lose your temper. Also, end every session with something your dog knows how to do. Start lessons indoors, where there are fewer distractions, until your dog understands the command, and then add those distractions.

Sit

The *sit* is a lovely command because if your dog is sitting, he is not bouncing around, wiggling, or running away from you. A sitting dog is easier to leash, for instance, when you're getting ready for a walk. A sit means that you can more easily control your dog when administering medicine, such as ear or eye drops.

How to Teach Sit

Teach your puppy to sit by luring him into position. Take a small treat and move it slowly back over his head. As he lifts his head to follow the treat, he will sink into a *sit*. The minute he sits, click and give him the treat.

Come

Teaching your Corgi to come is easy, and you can practice it many times during a day. There are two important things to

pads are already scented to encourage puppies to use them. If you plan to make an indoor area for your Corgi, you can get pads that fit into special holders, as well as washable pads.

Training Basic Obedience Commands

As you work with a clicker or marker word, there will come a "lightbulb moment" when you can see that your dog "gets it." He knows that he'll be rewarded for doing something, even if he isn't sure remember. First, never call your dog if you can't reinforce it. If he learns that he doesn't have to come, you won't be able to reliably get him to come when you want him. Second, never call your puppy for something unpleasant. Call him to feed him or to give him a toy or to pet him, but don't call him when you're going to cut his nails or give him medicine. At those times, go and get him. Otherwise, he will learn that coming to you results in negative things happening to him.

How to Teach Come

Start training by getting your puppy's attention. Call his name, pat your leg, and run backward. Your puppy will follow, and that's when you click and treat or praise and treat. Use a happy, high voice when you call him. Call him as you set down his food bowl. When you move your training outside, try calling him when he's playing. When he comes, give him his treat, then let him go back to playing. If you only call him when it's time

Stay is a useful command that can keep your dog out of trouble.

to stop playing, he'll be reluctant to come because he'll know that it will end his playtime.

Next, whenever he comes, take hold of his collar before you treat. There's no point in calling your dog if he just grabs his treat and runs away. You can include a *sit* at this point also, which will slow your dog down and help him focus on you.

Stay

Stay is a useful command that can help keep your Corgi out of trouble. You can put your Corgi in a *stay* to keep him away from the dinner table when you have guests. If you drop and break a glass, you can put your Corgi in a *stay* in another room while you clean up the broken pieces. A *stay* command will keep your dog from running out the front door when you go out to get the mail, and a dog in a *stay* has a moment to rest and calm down if a play session gets too rowdy.

All dogs should learn basic obedience commands.

How to Teach Stay

Start with your dog in a sitting position at your side. Put your hand, palm side facing your dog, in front of his nose, and tell him to stay. Take one step forward, at the same time turning to face your dog. Step back beside him. Praise and treat. At this point, you're not giving him much choice, and that's good. There's no room for error, and he is succeeding just by sitting there. The next step is to increase the distance. Take two steps forward before turning to face your dog. Gradually increase the distance. If your dog breaks the *stay*, calmly return him to the original spot and start again.

When your dog seems to understand the command, start walking around him to get back to your starting position. Walk to the left or right a few steps before returning to him and releasing him. Ask him to stay while he is in the *down* position. Don't be surprised if you have to start at the beginning because for your dog, this becomes an entirely different exercise.

Down

Down is a command like *sit* in that it can help you gain control of your dog. If you want him to remain in one spot for longer than a few minutes, *down* gives him a chance to relax yet still stay in one spot (after you've taught the *stay* command). If your dog is lying down, it may be easier to wipe off muddy toes or to give eye drops

Stay is a useful command that can help keep your Corgi out of trouble.

or clean ears. If, heaven forbid, your dog ever got loose and was across the street, giving the *down* command would keep him from running back across the street through traffic, and you could cross safely and snap on his leash.

How to Teach Down

Down is almost as easy to teach as *sit*. Get a small treat and have your dog sit. Then slowly move the treat down the front of your dog, and then out away from

With the **heel** command, your dog must walk next to you by your side.

If you have a flight of stairs, you can use them to help teach the *down*. Put your Corgi at the top of the steps and have him sit. Move your treat down below the level of the step. Your Corgi will lie down to be able to reach the treat on the step below.

Heel

Whether or not you have a fenced yard for exercise for your Corgi, he will need to know how to walk nicely on a lead. You don't want to carry him everywhere, and you want him to behave while on lead. It's no fun having a dog pulling you down the street or wrapping the lead around your legs. Your Corgi will need to heel formally, that is, walk on your left side, with his head level with your leg, if you plan to compete in rally or obedience, but otherwise, you may be satisfied if he walks quietly on a slack lead.

How to Teach Heel

Start with a collar. Your puppy may have arrived with a collar, but if not, get a soft cat collar or an adjustable nylon collar made for puppies. Most puppies will accept a collar with very little fuss beyond scratching at it a time or two. When you're ready to add a lead, attach it to the collar and let your puppy drag it around awhile. Always supervise this, as you don't want the lead to snag on something or for your puppy to get tangled in it. Again, most Corgis won't pay much attention to the

him. Technically, he should follow the treat, sliding into a *down*. My experience with Corgis is that they tend to stand up to follow the treat, so you'll need to try a different method. One is to cover the treat with your hand when the dog stands up. Let him paw, nuzzle, and nibble at your hand. Eventually, he will try lying down as a way to get at the treat. Immediately click and give him the treat. Corgis are clever enough to catch on after only a few repetitions.

Check It Out

TRAINING CHECKLIST

You'll need a:

✓ crate
✓ collar and lead
✓ designated area of your yard (for housetraining)
✓ schedule: your puppy will learn quickly if you have a schedule and stick to it; you might even want to print one out and post it on your refrigerator door
✓ collar and lead or a head halter: this is optional if you're indoors; outdoors, where there are more distractions, it can be helpful to have a collar and lead; if your yard isn't fenced, the collar and lead are essential
✓ clicker or a word that marks the action
✓ treats: teeny, tiny treats mean that your dog won't gain weight as he gains knowledge
✓ trainer, or a good book, or a DVD—or all three
✓ patience: never train when you're angry; if you can't be calm and happy, take a break

dragging lead. If it bothers your puppy, offer lots of treats and keep the training session short. Next, pick up the end of the lead and call your puppy, running backward as you did when teaching him to come. Follow him around while holding the lead. Don't try to guide or direct him. Just get him used to being attached to you.

None of this will take long at all. In fact, most Corgi puppies quickly accept collar, lead, and being attached. Move your training outside, and continue to follow your puppy, but this time, stop every few minutes. Don't say anything to the puppy—just stop. He will reach the end of the lead and look back in surprise. Stand

a moment and then start moving again. Repeat. Eventually, your puppy will start to understand that there's only forward motion when the lead is slack and also that he needs to keep an eye on you, as you are apt to stop without notice.

If you want your Corgi to stick to your left side in the *heel* position, use treats and drop them into his mouth only when he's beside you. If he forges ahead or pulls, stop moving. The *watch me* command can be useful to help keep your Corgi focused on you instead of on a squirrel or another dog. Say your puppy's name and the command "watch me," moving a treat up to beside your eyes. The minute you make eye contact,

Ask the Expert

CORGI TRAINING TIPS

— Pam Dennison is a member of the Association of Pet Dog Trainers (APDT) and the International Association of Animal Behavior Consultants (IAABC). She is the author of five training books, and speaks worldwide on training issues. Learn more about Pam at her website, www.positivedogs.com.

Q: Do you have any special hints or tips for training a Corgi?

A: Corgis are little, but they are a herding breed. That means that they don't take no for an answer, and they are high energy. So, they need exercise, but they also need a lot of mental stimulation as well. Do not wait to train your dog. Start when your puppy is eight weeks old. If he can't join a class, start clicker training yourself. Start at four to five weeks if you're near your breeder.

Your puppy will also need socialization with both people and with other dogs, or you may end up with behavioral problems. Sixteen to 20 weeks of age is the best time for socialization. Give your puppy a chance to do a lot of different things.

Veterinarian and breeder Lucy Jones adds that it is preferable if someone is home at least part of the day. If everyone's gone all day, it's hard on an intelligent breed, especially for a puppy. You have to make it up to them, but that doesn't mean spoiling them. A spoiled Corgi, like a spoiled child, turns into a monster. Your Corgi needs structure and rules, but you don't have to be controlling. It's not about control and discipline but about appreciation on both sides. Corgis like working with people and they enjoy figuring out what you want and how to do it, but the things you tell them have to make sense to them.

click and give the treat. You can practice this on or off lead, and once your Corgi understands, if he gets distracted on a walk, the *watch me* should have him turning his attention back to you.

The good news about both training for a slack lead and teaching your Corgi to watch you is that you can do both while you're enjoying your walk. It's a great way to keep your Corgi on his toes and to reinforce the proper behavior so that you are truly enjoying the walk and not arguing with a Corgi who is at the end of the lead and determined to catch that squirrel before it climbs a tree.

Finding a Trainer

Training methods have evolved over the years, and most people now agree that positive methods work as well or better than methods that use harsh corrections.

Food has become an accepted tool to use while training. So as you search for a trainer, keep in mind that you don't need a training collar, and you don't need to punish your Corgi for him to learn the behaviors you want to see.

One way to begin your search is to go to the Association of Pet Dog Trainers' (APDT) website at www.apdt.com. There you can enter your zip code and find any trainers in your area who are members of this organization. These trainers use positive methods, including clicker training. You can also call local boarding kennels and groomers. Sometimes trainers are affiliated with these facilities, but if not, they may be able to direct you to a trainer. Your local animal shelter may also be able to help.

Once you've found a trainer, ask to attend a class without your dog. If the trainer advocates hitting, pulling, or yelling at your dog, find another trainer.

If you can't find anyone in your area, many good training books and DVDs are available. I prefer a class because it gives your dog a chance to be out in public, and a class schedule makes me stick to my daily lessons—but training on your own is better than no training at all.

Chapter
7

Solving Problems
With Your
Pembroke Welsh Corgi

Dogs do many things because of instinct or just because they enjoy it. Many doggy activities release chemicals in the dog brain that make your Corgi feel good. Unfortunately, people don't always get the same joy out of doggy behaviors. Unless a particular behavior poses a threat, however, it is only a problem if it bothers someone. If I don't care if my dog destroys my lawn and digs holes everywhere, it's not a problem. For someone else who gardens or wants a smooth lawn, digging is a problem.

Barking (Excessive)

Let's start with barking. Corgis do bark. They are alert dogs and make excellent watchdogs. Unfortunately, they sometimes bark to tell you that a leaf has fallen. My own female recently barked at a caterpillar crawling across the back of a porch chair, and she always lets me know if there's a cat half a block away. Not all Corgis bark quite as much as Rhiannon does, but a barking Corgi is not uncommon. Barking is not something you can totally stop, but you can manage it so that you

Many problem behaviors can be solved with a little time and patience.

have some peace and quiet and the neighbors aren't complaining.

How to Manage It

If you tie your Corgi out, he will bark more than if you have a fenced yard, and he'll bark more if he can see through the fence than if the fence is solid. If you have a wire fence, consider planting bushes to help block your Corgi's view of the world. The bushes will also help muffle the barking. Even with a solid fence, your Corgi will know if someone, especially another dog, is on the other side, but the fence will prevent your dog from barking at everything he sees.

Indoors, limit your Corgi's access to windows. If your dog is allowed on the furniture, it won't take him long to figure out that he can have a comfortable seat from which to view the outside world, so arrange your furniture accordingly. At peak traffic times, such as when children are going to and from school, close the blinds or draw the drapes.

I have read that dogs are not as willing to bark if they are lying down, but none of my Corgis ever read that. They've all been just as happy to bark lying down, and Rhiannon has even barked while lying

PUPPIES AND PROBLEM BEHAVIORS

A dog's behavior isn't a problem unless it bothers someone, and most puppy behavior shouldn't bother you too much because he will outgrow most of those annoying behaviors. That doesn't mean that you should let your puppy chew nonstop on that antique chair or gnaw on your hand or dig indiscriminately in the yard, but it does mean that you won't have to deal with these behaviors forever.

You can, however, start to teach your puppy what you expect. Begin to teach him not to nip; don't wait until he's full grown. You can also teach a puppy not to jump, and the same goes for all of the behaviors listed in this chapter that may make you regard your puppy with something less than love.

Control your puppy firmly but gently. Distract him when necessary, and put him in his crate when you can't supervise his explorations, for his sake and yours. Chewing on an electric cord can be a fatal mistake.

If there are certain behaviors you don't want in your adult dog, don't encourage them in your puppy. It's easier to stop a habit from forming than to change it once it's formed. If you don't want your adult Corgi on the furniture, don't let that adorable puppy play on the couch. If the rule is no dogs on the bed, don't let your whining puppy sleep with you "just this once."

on her back. And she can bark, and does, with a toy in her mouth. Asking your dog to lie down, however, might change his focus from whatever he was barking at to you, so that might stop the barking.

You can also put barking on command, teaching your dog to "speak" and then teaching a *stop* command. Using your clicker or marker word, wait until your Corgi barks, then click and treat. (If you're not using a clicker, praise and treat). Once your dog has learned to bark on command, teach a *stop* command.

Use the word "stop," "enough," "quiet," or whatever word you're apt to say when your dog is barking. Rhiannon enjoys looking out the window, but she does know that if she starts to bark and I tell her to "stop it," she should stop barking and run to me for a treat. When she does come to me, I have her do a *down* briefly before we go into the kitchen to the treat jar. This helps shift her focus from outside to me and gives her a little time to calm down. If I treated her instantly, she might just run back to the window and start barking all over again.

If, for whatever reason, your Corgi just isn't stopping and you don't have the time to distract him (if you're on the phone, for example), then calmly put him in another room or in his crate for a brief time-out.

Chewing

Chewing isn't generally a problem with an adult Corgi, but it can be a problem with a puppy, especially if the puppy is teething. Chewing feels good during teething, and

If your puppy is chewing on inappropriate items, give him his own toy to chew.

puppies are happy to chew whatever is in reach.

How to Manage It

First, make sure that what is in reach is not your good leather shoes. Keep clothing out of reach of curious teething puppies. Don't leave your puppy unattended near the legs of antique furniture or the fringe of your oriental rug or around electrical cords. If you can't supervise your puppy, put him into his crate where he, as well as your possessions, will be safe.

Do supply your Corgi with nylon bones, such as Nylabones or hard rubber toys. If you can trust your puppy not to disembowel soft stuffed toys, those are fine as well. Knot an old towel or washcloth, wet it, and then put it in the freezer. When it has frozen, give it to your puppy. The cold will soothe his sore gums. Make sure that you supervise, though, so that your puppy doesn't bite off a chunk of towel and swallow it.

You can also give your dog a real bone, as long as it's not cooked. Never give any kind of cooked bone to your dog, as cooked bones can too easily splinter. Cow hooves are a popular chew treat for dogs, but they too can splinter, and it's been my experience that they smell. Some flavored chews may also stain carpeting, so be aware when you make your purchases.

Chewing is also something older dogs

enjoy, so even when your Corgi is beyond the teething stage, supply something appropriate for him to chew. Toys that can be stuffed with treats make good chew toys and also give your dog something to do when he's left alone.

Digging

Digging is another behavior most often seen in puppies, although adults will sometimes dig a hole in the summer as a place to lie in and be cool. Your Corgi may also dig at the openings to mole holes or other openings where there may be a critter of interest. If your Corgi is digging and it's just a passing puppy phase, you may not need to do anything more than supervise his time in the yard and divert his attention when he starts to dig. If you have an adult who has a passion for digging, you'll need to take other steps unless you are always outside with your Corgi and can distract him every time he starts to dig.

How to Manage It

A sandbox can make a good digging spot for your dog. You can make your own box, or buy a child's wading pool and fill it with sand. You can also just block off a section of your yard if you don't mind your dog digging there. Loosen the dirt so that he's encouraged to dig in an easier spot than the rest of your lawn. Once you've created a digging pit, bury some

If your dog is digging in the yard, try giving him his own spot to dig to keep your garden safe.

tasty treats just under the surface to entice your Corgi to dig in that spot and no other. Initially, go out with your dog, and if he starts to dig somewhere other than the designated spot, call him to the correct spot, praise, and dig a little yourself to give him the idea. Praise him when he digs in the correct spot.

Depending on your dog's temperament, just a reprimand may stop him from digging, and you won't even need a special pit. My parents' Corgi had a very soft temperament. My father caught him digging up the lawn one day and scolded

Ask the Expert

MANAGING SERIOUS PROBLEM BEHAVIORS

— Pam Dennison

Q: When would you recommend calling in a professional trainer? Nipping is a Corgi trait, from herding cattle. It's like a terrier digging. You might not be able to totally stop it. How would you manage it?

A: I like to teach the *excuse me* cue. This teaches the dog to yield if you step toward him. This helps with both jumping and nipping because when you say "Excuse me," the dog backs up. If your dog is nipping at your heels as you go up or down the stairs, throw treats ahead of you. Use only positive methods and never, ever hit or kick your dog. If your dog is truly aggressive, seek professional help immediately.

Another point to remember is that growling is good. Growling is a warning. Dogs can't tell you when they're frightened or angry, but they can growl. If you teach a dog not to growl, you remove the warning. If your dog is growling, remove him from the situation before the growl escalates into a bite.

him, saying "No digging" in his sternest voice. Not only did Merlin never dig again, but we couldn't even say the word anymore without him looking crestfallen. We had to spell it so that we wouldn't hurt his feelings.

House Soiling

I am not talking about puppy accidents here, as those are to be expected and will end once your puppy is housetrained. In the case of house soiling, I'm talking about problems with an adult dog who has been housetrained but who is now eliminating in the house.

How to Manage It

Submissive wetting is generally seen in younger dogs and is the dog's way of saying that he recognizes you as the boss. It's also more apt to occur if the dog is very excited. So if you have a dog who wets (frequently accompanied by rolling over on his back) whenever you come home, don't give an effusive greeting, and don't yell, which will just make things worse. Enter the house calmly and don't pay attention to the dog. Move quietly. You can greet your dog, but don't pet him or roughhouse with him. One of our females used to wet when we had company. We made sure that we took her out to eliminate just before company was expected and told our guests to ignore her. If we didn't have a chance to take her out, we'd crate her until the guests were in and the dog was calm. She eventually outgrew the habit.

Rule Out a Physical Problem

If you have an older dog who has always been reliable in the house, a veterinary exam is the first step to rule out any physical problems. Older dogs, especially spayed females, may tend to dribble urine, and there are medicines that can help with this problem. If a veterinary checkup reveals no physical causes, consider your routine. Have things changed in the household? Dogs are creatures of habit, and if your dog is no longer getting a break at a specific time, he may go anyway, just because he's used to going at that time. Or your senior dog may just not be able to hold it for as long as he used to.

If a new pet, especially another dog, has been added to the family, your dog may be marking his territory. With a dog who is marking his territory, you may have to confine him in his crate or in the kitchen or bathroom when you can't watch him. If he's not already neutered, that operation may help lessen his desire to mark, but there's no guarantee.

Confine Your Dog

A senior dog may also need to be confined. Bring out your baby gate from his youth and spread out papers, which will make cleanup a bit easier. If your schedule permits, take him out more often. A dog who has gone out every six to eight hours may need to go out every four, or three, or even two hours. My senior dog is limited to our kitchen and laundry room area when I can't watch him. I spread out newspapers in one area, and he always goes there, making it easy to spot, as well as easy to clean up. In fact, now, even if the door is open to the carpeted living room, Griffin goes on the paper. A mop with a disposable pad makes floor cleaning quick and easy. Griffin goes out about every two hours.

When the problem first began, Griffin went more often indoors than out, but as with housetraining a puppy, the senior dog needs a routine. I've discovered that he needs to go more often in the morning, so I give him the opportunity to go out every hour to hour and a half. In the afternoon, this stretches to about three hours. Griffin is getting more and more dependable in the house, but he will never be totally reliable again. So when we're out, he's confined. Yes, it's a bit more work, but not much, and dogs are still less work than children.

One little hint: The ink from the newspapers does come off. We discovered

If you don't want your Corgi to jump up on guests, put him in another room or have him perform a *sit* as they arrive.

that we were walking over dry newspaper and then tracking ink onto our light-colored carpet. We've switched to the end rolls of clean paper from our local newspaper printing plant. If you have a newspaper in your area, see if they give away or sell the end rolls. They're not expensive, and they can save your carpeting.

Jumping Up

Many Corgis like to jump up, and many Corgi owners don't mind. When Rhiannon's paws are on my knees, I can pet her easily without bending all the way over. I do not, however, want her jumping up when I'm dressed to go out, and visitors who aren't dog people don't want her jumping on them. If she were to jump up on the small children next door, she could easily knock them over, and the same is true if your Corgi jumps up on an older person who may be a bit unsteady on her feet.

How to Manage It

If you don't care if your Corgi jumps, teach him to jump on cue. Friends with two Golden Retrievers use the word "hug" and their dogs jump up. Use any word you want and then your Corgi will jump up when you want him to and not when his paws are wet and muddy.

If you don't want your Corgi jumping at all, first make sure that everyone in the family is in agreement. It's not fair to the dog if one person is encouraging him to jump and someone else is scolding him for it. The best method for teaching your Corgi not to jump up is to turn sideways and ignore him. Only acknowledge him when all four paws are on the floor. While it's true that some dogs will be deterred by a harsh tone of voice, many dogs don't care what kind of attention they get, as long as they get attention. If you reward your Corgi with attention, even if it's a scolding, he will continue to jump up. By turning away and ignoring him, you are depriving him of attention.

Another method is to just manage the situation. There are no small children in our home, and I like Rhiannon to jump up, so when my mother visits, I put Rhiannon upstairs until my mother is seated and comfortable. Then I let Rhiannon out. She can greet my mother by putting her paws on my mother's knees, and my mother can easily pet her that way.

Nipping

Nipping should not be confused with biting. Nipping doesn't break the skin and is not generally an aggressive action. That doesn't mean that it can't hurt, and it can definitely be annoying. Corgis were bred to herd cattle, and part of that herding includes nipping the cattle on the heels. A Corgi will instinctively chase and nip. If you don't have cattle or sheep in your backyard, those playing children will do just as well. If those children run faster and add screaming to the scenario, your Corgi will run faster too and nip harder.

How to Manage It

Teaching a Corgi not to nip is like teaching a terrier not to dig. It's an uphill battle.

Adult Nipping

First, explain to any children that the dog is not trying to bite them. Second, tell them that if the dog chases them to stop moving. You can also remove the dog from the yard during playtime. Because both children and dog may enjoy playing together, use some distracting techniques to discourage your Corgi from nipping. Throw a ball, toy, or tasty treat across his path. If the game involves a ball, that will probably be enough of a distraction, as many Corgis enjoy a good game of fetch or playing for both teams with a soccer ball.

Attach a long piece of clothesline to his collar so that you can stop his behavior from a distance. (Never leave your Corgi unattended while a rope or lead is attached to his collar, as it could easily snag on a tree or bush and your Corgi could be injured.) Unless you and your Corgi are actually herding, most Corgis outgrow the constant chasing and nipping. If none of your efforts make an impression, contact a trainer who understands herding breeds.

Puppy Nipping

Another kind of nipping is the playful nipping of a puppy. Those puppy teeth are sharp, and even a playful nip can hurt. If your puppy nips you during a play session, use a high-pitched voice and yelp. When your puppy was with his littermates, a yelp or squeal from a sibling meant that he had bitten too hard. Your

Corgi will understand your yelp just as he understood his sibling's. Whenever your puppy puts his teeth on you, yelp. If he doesn't take the hint, stop the play session for a few minutes and ignore him. If he needs a time-out, calmly put him in his crate. He'll soon learn that putting his mouth on a person ends the game. Playing with toys, rather than using your hands, will also redirect those sharp little teeth.

Some dog breeds like to have something

If your puppy nips you during a play session, use a high-pitched voice and yelp to get him to stop.

in their mouths more than others. Corgis are not generally "mouthy," but my female is. Rhiannon likes to use her mouth to see what's going on. When she wakes me up in the morning, she takes my hand in her mouth. There's no pressure, but my hand is in her mouth. I couldn't stop Rhiannon from using her mouth, but having a strange dog grab your hand is not reassuring to visitors, so I taught Rhiannon to get her toy. When I say "Get your toy," she immediately runs to find the toy and then returns to any guests. She keeps the toy in her mouth and can easily be petted while she's holding her toy.

Many people teach their dog to go lie down in a specific spot when guests arrive. You can do this with your Corgi as well, and this prevents jumping up as well as any inclination to grab a hand.

When to Seek Professional Help

The odds are that you will never need to seek professional behavioral help for your Corgi. Corgis, as a breed, have good temperaments and get along well with people and other animals. A professional trainer is always a good idea, however, because she can help you get the best out of your dog and teach you effective methods for training your Corgi. A good trainer can even help with some attitude problems, including the ones listed in this chapter. But there may come a time when

PROBLEM BEHAVIOR CHECKLIST

You'll need many of the items listed in the chapter on training:

✓ crate
✓ good book on positive training
✓ lead and collar
✓ patience
✓ professional trainer (optional)
✓ treats
✓ your breeder's phone number

you need more help than a trainer can give.

Seek professional help if your dog growls, snaps, or bites for no reason, and don't delay. First, have your veterinarian give your dog a full physical. In older dogs, especially, arthritis or some other ailment may be causing pain, which in turn can make your dog snap or bite. Even a younger dog can have a physical problem. Once you've ruled out a physical cause, you may need an animal behaviorist. The best place to start your search is by asking your veterinarian for a referral. Members of your local kennel club may also be a good source of information. There is no national standard for certification as an animal behaviorist, so consider credentials and ask for references. If you can't find a behaviorist locally, try one of these websites:

- www.animalbehavior.org: This is the site for the Animal Behavior Society (ABS), a professional organization for the study of animal behavior. Members must hold degrees in psychology, biology, zoology, or animal science. They must also have demonstrated expertise in the principles of animal behavior.
- www.avsabonline.org/avsabonline/: The American Veterinary Society of Animal Behavior (AVSAB) is a group of veterinarians that treats problem behaviors in animals.
- www.iaabc.org: Another source is the International Association of Animal Behavior Consultants (IAABC). Members have diverse backgrounds, but all have the knowledge and skill needed to work with families and their dogs.

It's unlikely that you'll ever need this level of help with your Corgi, but if you do have a problem, don't hesitate to get professional help. The earlier you do, the more likely the problem can be solved.

Chapter
8

Activities With Your
Pembroke Welsh Corgi

C orgis like to keep busy, and a great way to keep your Corgi busy and enjoy his company is to participate in some kind of doggy sport. There are plenty to choose from, and there's nothing to stop you from doing more than one. And while you can practice many activities in the privacy of your own home and yard, to compete, you'll need to travel, so this chapter includes how to get there from here.

Despite their short legs, Corgis are very good at agility.

Sports

If you've decided that you want to show your Corgi or want to compete in performance events, you'll be on the road most weekends. Bring food, water, and a first-aid kit, and you may want to add another crate or two if you'll be shuttling between a motel room and an event site. Maybe you'll add a tack box and a grooming table. It can be lots of fun spending the weekends with your Corgi and with other like-minded dog people.

Agility

Don't let those short legs fool you—Corgis are very good at agility. Agility requires your dog to go over, around, and through multiple obstacles in a specific amount of time. There are tunnels, teeter-totters, jumps, and weave poles, and depending on the level, there are varying degrees of difficulty. The American Kennel Club (AKC) offers agility, as does the United Kennel Club (UKC) and two other major organizations, the United States Dog Agility Association (USDAA) and the North American Dog Agility Club (NADAC), also sanction agility events. The Australian Shepherd Club of America (ASCA) allows all breeds to compete, and a new organization, Canine Performance Events (CPE), offers standard agility as well as several games. While the basic pieces of equipment are similar, the rules vary with each organization, so make

THE PAL/ILP

If conformation shows don't appeal to you, there are lots of performance events to try. If your Corgi doesn't have registration papers, you can still compete with a special number. With the AKC, for instance, after filling out forms and submitting them with photos of your dog, you will be given a PAL/ILP number. This stands for Purebred Alternative Listing/Indefinite Listing Privilege, and it will allow you to compete in AKC performance events.

---

sure that you know those rules before you compete. Your Corgi will need to be at least 18 months old to compete in all but CPE, which has a 15-month age limit.

Canine Freestyle

If *Dancing with the Stars* is one of your favorite television programs, try dancing with your Corgi. The Canine Freestyle Federation (CFF) places the emphasis on skill, with specific moves a required part of a routine. The handler may not dance alone or touch the dog. The World Canine Freestyle Organization (WCFO) is less strict, and handlers have more leeway in costumes and choreography.

Conformation (Dog Shows)

Conformation shows are the shows you see on television. If your Corgi meets the standard and is registered with a show-sanctioning organization, such as the AKC, the UKC, or the Canadian Kennel Club (CKC), you might want to try to earn his championship. If this is your

first Corgi, talk to your breeder about whether he is show quality. Join a local kennel club and attend handling classes. You'll learn how to *gait* your dog, which means moving him around a ring at a trot. You'll learn to *stack* him, which means getting him to stand properly both on the ground and on a table, where the judge will examine him for proper structure. To become a champion, your dog must earn 15 points. A dog can earn from one to five points at a show, with a major being a win of three, four, or five points. Your dog must win two majors as part of those 15 points. For complete information on conformation showing, check out the AKC's website.

Herding Trials

If you want to let your Corgi do what he was bred to do, herding trials are the way to do it. The AKC, CKC, ASCA, and the American Herding Breeds Association (AHBA) all offer herding trials, with a chance to just test your dog's instincts or go all the way to earning a herding championship, depending on which organization's trials you attend. Sometimes it takes two or three tries before your Corgi's instincts kick in, so don't give up if your Corgi doesn't show any interest in sheep (or ducks or cattle) the first time he sees them.

Obedience

AKC obedience is a bit more structured of an event and has several levels, ranging

Obedience is a more structured event in which dogs must perform certain obedience commands.

from CD (Companion Dog) to UDX (Utility Dog Excellent). Your dog will need to know how to heel, sit, down, stay, and at higher levels, retrieve a dumbbell, jump both high and broad jumps, and identify specific articles that you have handled. Each exercise is assigned a specific number of points, with the total of all of the exercises adding up to 200. Your dog needs to earn at least 50 percent of each exercise, with a total score of 170 points or better to qualify and earn a green ribbon, and your dog needs to qualify three times to earn a title.

Rally

Rally is a good way to ease into obedience, as it's a little more relaxed. You are allowed to give multiple commands and can talk to your dog as much as you like. Depending on the level of competition, there are 10 to 20 stations in rally. At each station, a card lists instructions, such as "down" or "stand for examination." Once you complete the exercise, you move on to the next station.

Tracking

Tracking is a bit slower paced, and your dog either passes or fails on a track. The AKC offers three tracking titles: TD or Tracking Dog, TDX or Tracking Dog Excellent, and VST or Variable Surface Tracker. The level of difficulty increases, but at all levels your dog must be able to

Puppy Love

TRAVELING WITH A PUPPY

If you're traveling with a puppy, your checklist will be the same as that for an adult, but keep in mind that a puppy may need more frequent rest stops than an adult dog, and a puppy may also need more frequent meals. Take along more cleaning supplies and more towels, too, as the stress of traveling may mean that your puppy has an accident or two. Puppies can sometimes become carsick as well, so if you know ahead of time that you'll be traveling with your puppy, get him used to car rides by taking short drives, and keep the rides enjoyable. If every ride ends at the vet's, your puppy won't be an enthusiastic traveler.

If you're planning to show your puppy in conformation, he'll need to be six months old before you can enter him in a show. Your puppy will need to be 6 months old to compete in rally or obedience as well, and for most other performance events, 18 months is the youngest a dog can be to participate.

follow a track, which includes turns, possibly obstacles, and—with variable surface tracking—different surfaces, such as pavement, gravel, sand, and vegetation. Along the way, your dog must locate and identify articles made of metal, plastic, leather, or cloth. You don't need much equipment for tracking, aside from some space to lay tracks, and you don't need to depend on anyone else. When you want to practice, just put the harness on your dog and go.

Therapy Work

Maybe you like to be with your Corgi, but you're not very competitive. In fact, the phrase "couch potato" is descriptive. If you like the idea of helping others, maybe you and your Corgi have a career as a

therapy team. Therapy dogs visit hospitals and other health care facilities, so your Corgi needs to be calm and friendly. He can't bark at wheelchairs or at people on crutches, and if someone pets him a bit roughly or tugs at a leg or an ear, he can't growl or snap.

People who are serious about therapy work generally get their dogs certified with Therapy Dogs International or the Delta Society. These organizations require dogs to pass a test similar to the Canine Good Citizen test offered by the AKC. If your Corgi passes the test, he'll get an ID tag for his collar, and you'll get a wallet card showing that your dog is a certified therapy dog. Depending on the organization, you may also have insurance coverage, and you'll also get information on what to do when making a therapy dog visit.

School visits are another good way for you and your Corgi to connect with people. See if your local school system has a reading program that uses dogs. Many children who find reading a challenge will happily read to a canine buddy. A woman I know uses her Corgi in such a program, and after the reading session, the student is allowed to walk the dog through the halls.

Traveling With Your Corgi

It's always fun to be able to take your Corgi with you when you travel, but there are some things to consider. First is your dog's safety. And no matter where you're traveling, take a copy of your dog's health records and any medication he may need. You may also want to pack a small first-aid kit. Pack enough food for the entire trip; don't assume that your brand will be found everywhere. Take water from home, and gradually mix it with the water at

If your dog is not the athletic type, therapy work might be perfect for him.

If you're traveling on a long journey with your Corgi by car, be sure to give him plenty of breaks to stretch his legs.

your location. This will help prevent any problems from unfamiliar water. Take a lead and collar, and make sure that your dog has ID tags. Having your cell phone number on his tag is a good idea.

Car Travel

Dogs should not ride in a car unrestrained. If there's an accident, they can become a flying object, leading to harm for both the dog and possibly a passenger. Also, the risk is too great that a dog will escape when someone opens a door. Nothing will ruin your vacation faster than losing your dog at a rest stop.

The best method of restraint is a crate, and that crate should rest on the floor behind a front seat. If you need to put the crate on a seat, make sure that it is securely fastened with special straps or with a seat belt. Soft mesh crates don't offer much protection. Wire crates are better, but solid plastic crates are the best. You can use a smaller crate than you might use at home, but your dog should still be able to sit, stand, and turn around comfortably.

Accustom Your Corgi to the Car

If your Corgi is not already used to rides in the car, take him for short, happy rides before your long trip. A drive to the vet's doesn't count! Most dogs are happy travelers, but if your Corgi hesitates to get in the car, take it slow. Be patient. First, with the doors to the car open on both sides, coax your Corgi in with treats. Don't try to keep him in the car if he doesn't want to stay. After a few of these sessions, close the doors on one side. Lure him in and pet him. Feed him some more treats. Throw treats into the crate and close him in briefly. Next, take a short drive around the block. Always keep the experience

SPORTS AND SAFETY

Corgis are tough little dogs, but they can overdo things, so it's up to you to keep your furry athlete safe. Don't push young dogs, whose bones and muscles are still growing. Limit the height of jumps for young dogs, as well as keeping training sessions short. Make sure that there's always water available. On hot days, a child's wading pool filled with water can help keep your Corgi cool after an agility run or some herding practice.

Help your dog stretch and warm up before a competition. A dog who goes directly from a crate to an activity risks injury. A good stretching exercise is to have your Corgi put his front paws up on your legs. Walk and trot your Corgi so that he can stretch and warm up. If he will be jumping, have him go over a few low jumps. See if he'll have a drink of water.

Water should always be available, but don't feed your Corgi a big meal before a competition. Corgis as a breed aren't prone to stomach torsion, but a full stomach and heavy physical activity increases the chances of the stomach turning over and sealing off the openings to the esophagus and the intestine—a life-threatening emergency. If, while practicing, your Corgi does injure himself, stop immediately. (If you are competing, the judge will stop you.) Continuing to work will only aggravate an injury and can turn a minor problem into something serious.

Finally, keep your Corgi on lead when not actually competing. Even the best-trained dogs can wander into dangerous situations or get lost. Keeping your Corgi safe keeps competition fun.

pleasant and use lots of treats. Corgis are generally so food motivated that it shouldn't take long before your dog is happily hopping into the car.

Never Leave Your Corgi in the Car

No matter how long or short a ride you're taking with your Corgi, remember not to leave him in a hot car. Even with the windows partly open, a car in the sun in summer can quickly reach killing temperatures. Also, remember that shade moves. You may have parked under a shady tree in the morning, but by mid-afternoon, your car may be in direct sunlight. If you can't guarantee a cool place for your dog, it may be best to leave him home.

Air Travel

You may, of course, be flying to your vacation destination, and that requires different thought. Every airline is different and the rules change frequently, so check with your specific carrier so that there'll be no surprises. All airlines have limits on when they will fly dogs as cargo, and some may have a limit as to how many they will accept on any given flight.

Get an Airline-Approved Crate

If your dog will be flying as baggage, you will need an airline-approved crate. Plastic may be a better bet than metal because metal tends to absorb more heat. Tape a label on the crate that lists

Traveling with your Corgi on a vacation can be an unforgettable experience

the destination, your name, address, and telephone number, and the dog's name. You might also want to include your veterinarian's phone number. Make sure that there is absorbent bedding in the crate. Freeze water in the water dish so that your dog can either lick the ice or drink the water as the ice melts. This will prevent the water supply from spilling all at once. You may also want to run a bungee cord over the door to prevent it from opening if the crate is dropped.

Ask Questions of Airline Personnel

Check with airline personnel about how and when your dog will be loaded and where and when you can pick him up when the flight lands. Plan your route carefully. Plane transfers will be harder on your dog, especially if the plane heats up or the crate is left on the blacktop in the sun. There is also more of a chance that he can get lost en route. If you are traveling in very hot weather, the airline may refuse to fly your dog at all. The optimal temperature range and frequently the range the airlines use is 45° to 85°F (7.2° to 29.4°C). If it will be colder than 45°F (7.2°C) or warmer than 85°F (29.4°F) at the originating airport, your destination, or anyplace in between where the plane may land, most airlines will refuse to ship your dog.

If you don't actually see your dog being boarded, ask the gate counter agent to

If your dog will be flying as baggage, you will need an airline-approved crate.

Ask the Expert

PERFORMANCE ACTIVITY TIPS

—Julia Clough, Corgi breeder

Q: What have you done with your Corgis? Any tips for beginners on training a Corgi for performance activities?

A: I've put titles on my Corgis in conformation, obedience, rally, agility, herding, and tracking. I'm very proud of the fact that five of my dogs have earned the Lila Wolfman Achievement Award from the Mayflower Pembroke Welsh Corgi Club. This means that the dog has a conformation championship, a CD, and one other performance title. I like to introduce my dogs to everything on a fun basis. It shouldn't be work; they should enjoy what they do. I do like to test all my dogs in herding. I'd say that everything revolves around obedience. Go to whatever class is convenient, and go on a regular basis. Ground the puppy in the basics. After that, explore whatever performance events interest you. Your Corgi will love it. They need a job, and they need and want to interact with humans.

call the ramp to make sure that your dog is on board. Pick up the dog promptly at your destination. If you don't get your dog in a reasonable amount of time, ask about it. Ask before your plane has taken off again.

Airline Regulations

Some Corgis may be small enough for soft carriers that will fit under the seat in the cabin. Airlines generally limit the number of live animals they will allow in the passenger section, and they charge for this service, so make your arrangements ahead of time. Don't just arrive at the airport with your dog in his carrier.

Also, the last time I flew, there was a metal box bolted to the floor, which gave me my very own video monitor but which also took up a good part of the under-seat space. I'm not sure I could have crammed a pet carrier into the remaining space. Taking a Corgi into the passenger area may not be an option on some planes.

If you've decided that you do want to try to take your dog on the plane with you, make sure that he's used to the carrier before the trip. Feed him in the carrier. Take him on short car rides in the carrier. If he's crate trained, you shouldn't have too much trouble, but the soft dog carriers are smaller than crates, so there will be a bit of adjustment necessary.

Another point to consider when flying

Check It Out

ACTIVITIES AND TRAVEL CHECKLIST

Your travel and activities checklist will vary, depending on what you are doing, but it could look something like this:

✓ entry forms if entered in an event
✓ exercise pen
✓ first-aid kit
✓ food and water, and bowls
✓ grooming supplies
✓ identification
✓ leash and collar (harness and tracking lead, if tracking)
✓ medical records
✓ towels, both cloth and paper
✓ travel crate

is whether or not a quarantine is required at your destination. Britain used to have a six-month quarantine, which they no longer have if your dog meets certain vaccination requirements. Hawaii's quarantine time has recently been shortened. Know what the regulations are before you arrive at your destination.

Pet Airways is another option for flying your dog. This airline flies only dogs and cats (known as "pawsengers"). The rates are comparable to other airlines, but because the animals fly in the cabin, there's no worry about outside temperatures. The only people on board are the pilot and the flight attendant, who is usually a veterinary technician. Each pet has his own carrier. The airline has hubs in Farmingdale, New York; Fort Lauderdale, Florida; Chicago; Boulder, Colorado; and Los Angeles, with plans for 20 more locations by 2012.

Lodging

Make sure that your dog will be welcome wherever you're traveling. If you're staying with friends or family, don't assume that they'll welcome your Corgi with open arms. If your final destination is a motel, make sure that pets are allowed. The same goes for campgrounds. Find out what the regulations are before you arrive. It's no fun trying to find a new place to stay at the last minute because your Corgi isn't welcome.

The same goes for any place you may be staying en route. AAA offers members a book of pet-friendly motels, hotels, and campgrounds, *Traveling With Your Pet*. Some places charge an extra fee for pets, so take that into consideration as you make your reservations, and remember to double-check with a phone call, as regulations and fees may have changed since the book was published.

Make sure that your dog will be welcome wherever you're traveling.

No matter where you stay with your dog, be a responsible dog owner. Always pick up after your dog. If he enjoys sleeping on the bed with you, cover the spread with a sheet that you've brought along to keep dirt and dog hair from working into the spread. Keep your dog crated in motel rooms when you're not there. Turn on the television or a radio to mask sounds that might start your dog barking.

If You Can't Take Your Corgi With You

Sometimes it may be better for everyone to either board your dog or hire a pet sitter. Yes, it's hard to leave your Corgi behind, but most Corgis adjust well to kennels, especially if the operator offers a treat or two. You can enjoy your vacation without having to care for your dog, and your dog will be safe.

Chapter
9

Health of Your
Pembroke Welsh Corgi

C orgis generally live 12 to 14 years, with some living to be 16 or older, but they can't do it alone. They need good food, regular exercise, contact with people, and a good veterinarian to administer vaccinations, offer an annual exam, and be there for emergencies.

Finding a Veterinarian

If you've had a dog before, you already have a veterinarian, but if this is your first

If this is your first dog, you'll need to acquire a vet.

dog, you'll need to choose a vet. Ideally, you should start your search before you get your Corgi puppy. Otherwise, try to find one soon for that first visit. You want to make sure that your puppy gets a clean bill of health right away, and depending on the age of your puppy, he may be in need of vaccinations.

Distance may be a factor in choosing your vet. You may not mind a drive for routine visits, but in an emergency, you might wish that you'd chosen a practice closer to home. Ask how a practice handles emergencies. Is someone on call? Is there more than one doctor in the practice? A small practice means that the veterinarian will know your dog well because she will see him at every visit, but if there's an emergency and your veterinarian is unavailable, the veterinarian you do visit won't have any of your pet's medical history. In a larger practice, while you may not always see the same doctor every time, your dog's medical records will be available to every doctor in the practice.

Consider what kind of care you want your dog to have. If you like the idea of natural remedies, make sure that your veterinarian can offer that kind of care. If possible, visit the office. The waiting room should be clean, and there should be enough space so that all the clients are not crowded together.

Find someone you are comfortable with

Your puppy will need to see the vet within the first few days that you've acquired him.

who will talk to you about your pet's care and who will answer your questions. No veterinarian will know your dog as well as you do. Ideally, you and your veterinarian will be partners working together to keep your dog healthy.

The Annual Checkup

You should make an appointment at least once a year for a general checkup for your Corgi. This is when vaccinations will be updated. Your veterinarian will give your

Corgi a physical exam as well, looking at his eyes, into his ears, and checking his mouth and throat to see if there's anything out of the ordinary. The vet will listen to his heart and lungs and palpate your dog's abdomen to see if there are any growths. For an annual exam, you may be asked for a fecal sample so that the staff can determine if your dog has any internal parasites. There may be a blood test for heartworm, and at this time, you'll get your next prescription of heartworm

PUUPPY HEALTH

You're not going to have many health worries with a normal puppy who is up to date on vaccinations, but that doesn't mean that you don't need to think about his health. Feed a top-quality food and start getting your puppy used to having his teeth brushed. Keep cupboard doors closed, and make sure your puppy can't get into cleaning products or into any food. Even foods that aren't toxic can make your puppy ill if he eats too much. Supervise your puppy's exploring so that he doesn't munch on an electric cord or end up eating something that could mean surgery. As your puppy grows, schedule annual vet visits to make sure that he has a clean bill of health and to catch any problems early.

Remember that human interaction and exercise are just as important as good food and regular checkups. Take the proper precautions and then enjoy your puppy.

preventive. If there's tartar buildup on your dog's teeth, he may be scheduled for a dental cleaning. Your Corgi will also be weighed, and the veterinarian may recommend a diet. If you have any questions or concerns, this is the time to get the answers.

Vaccinations

Depending on the age of your puppy, he may or may not have received his first set of vaccinations. Many veterinarians give the first set of shots at 8 weeks, then 12 weeks, 16 weeks, and then annually after that, although some veterinarians may also recommend shots at 18 to 20 weeks and then annually. Check with the breeder to see which, if any, shots have been given to your puppy.

Vaccinations have become a topic of conversation because many veterinarians and breeders now feel that annual vaccinations are unnecessary. Dr. Jean Dodds recommends specific puppy shots and shots at a year old and then none after that. Many breeders give vaccinations every three years until the dog is between seven and ten and then nothing after that.

If you want to measure your Corgi's level of immunity, have your dog's *titer* checked. A titer is a measurement of a substance in solution—in this case, the amount of antibodies found in the blood. Some people check titers annually and others every few years.

Talk to your breeder about vaccinations as well as to your veterinarian. You need to do what you feel comfortable with, as well as meet whatever local or state requirements there may be. An inoculation against rabies is required in every state, but the time span between shots may differ. Some states require a rabies shot every year and others every three years. Check with your veterinarian for your state's requirements.

Combination shots that are generally given to puppies include distemper, leptospirosis, hepatitis, parvovirus, and may or may not also include parainfluenza. Your veterinarian may also recommend shots against Lyme disease and coronavirus. If you plan to board your dog, the kennel may require a bordetella shot as well.

The following are some diseases that dogs are commonly vaccinated against:

Bordetella (Kennel Cough)

Bordetella, often called kennel cough, is an airborne infection that spreads quickly. It causes a dry, hacking cough and responds well to antibiotics. Or it may also run its course with no treatment at all in about two weeks. In a healthy dog, it is not likely to cause any permanent damage or to be fatal, although the disease is worse in puppies than in adults. There are more than 100 different strains of bordetella, and not all are covered by the vaccine.

Coronavirus

Coronavirus is a highly contagious virus that results in diarrhea for about a week.

Most dogs recover without treatment, but in cases of severe dehydration, the dog may require intravenous fluids.

Distemper

Distemper is a dangerous disease that has a very low recovery rate. The danger from this very contagious virus is greatest in dogs three to six months of age and in dogs over six years of age. Symptoms include vomiting, coughing, and fever, and death is the usual outcome.

Regular health care will help your Corgi live a longer, healthier life.

Hepatitis

Hepatitis is a viral disease that attacks the liver and may also affect other organs. There are two forms: acute and severe. Symptoms in acute hepatitis include fever, vomiting, and diarrhea. The dog may also have swollen lymph nodes, pale gums, and yellowish eyes. There is no treatment, but the dog will probably recover within a couple of weeks. With the severe form of the disease, bloody vomit and diarrhea and bloody gums are symptoms. Again, there is no treatment, and infected dogs frequently die.

Leptospirosis

Leptospirosis is a bacteria frequently transmitted through urine, especially that of rats and mice. A dog with leptospirosis may vomit, be lethargic, have muscle pain, and may have diarrhea or blood in the urine. There may be abdominal pain. Penicillin is used to treat the disease, and the dog may also be given intravenous fluids.

Lyme Disease

The deer tick spreads Lyme disease. Ask your vet if this disease is a problem in your area. Deer ticks are tiny critters, so you might not ever see one, but if your dog contracts Lyme disease, he may be stiff or lame and have swollen joints. Treatment for the disease is a course of antibiotics for four weeks.

Parvovirus

Parvovirus is another disease that may be fatal, especially if the symptoms include vomiting and bloody diarrhea. There may be a fever, and the dog will be lethargic and depressed. Dogs with mild cases of the disease generally recover, but young puppies are very susceptible and generally do not survive. Parvovirus is treated with hydration and antibiotics.

Rabies

Rabies is a virus that attacks the central nervous system of mammals and is spread through saliva. Common carriers in the wild include bats, foxes, raccoons, and skunks. Once symptoms appear, there is no cure and the disease is fatal. A rabid animal may be shy or aggressive. He may snap or bite, may seem nervous, may wander aimlessly, be very excited, or may seem disoriented. The animal may have seizures or paralysis of the throat muscles that may make it impossible to

FIRST-AID KIT

There is always the chance of an accident, so be prepared with some basic knowledge of dog first aid. Your local Red Cross may offer a course in pet first aid. If you suspect that your dog may have gotten into something poisonous, call the ASPCA National Animal Poison Control Center at 1-800-548-2423. Have your credit card ready, as there is a consulting fee. Or call 1-900-680-0000 and the charges will be added to your phone bill.

Keep some basic first-aid supplies on hand. People and dog first-aid items are similar, so you may already have many of these items in your medicine cabinet. You should have a roll of gauze, some gauze pads, baby aspirin, Betadine, hydrogen peroxide, Kaopectate, a thermometer, tweezers, and your veterinarian's phone number. A blanket can make moving an injured dog easier and safer and should be used to keep him warm if he is in shock. A dog in pain will snap and bite at anything, even your loving hands, so a muzzle will protect you and make it easier to treat and transport your dog. You might consider buying a nylon muzzle from a pet supply store or catalog, or you can use a length of gauze from the roll in the first-aid kit. Never muzzle a dog who is having trouble breathing. If there is danger of a bite, cover the dog's head with a blanket while you are examining him. It may not prevent a bite, but it may help.

With any emergency, if possible, take the time to call ahead and alert your veterinarian and his staff to the emergency. They can then be ready for your arrival, and no time will be wasted.

swallow. The animal may salivate heavily and may have a fever.

Spaying and Neutering

Between six months and two years, besides finishing off the growth period, your dog will become sexually mature. Spaying or neutering can eliminate some of the manifestations of sexual maturity, and certainly this is the best approach if you are not seriously committed to showing or breeding.

Depending on where you live, you may have already encountered fleas or ticks (pictured).

infections, as well as the twice yearly "season."

Parasites

Parasites, both internal and external, live off their host, which means that they are stealing nutrients your dog needs. They may also cause secondary problems. For instance, your dog may develop skin sores as a result of digging and scratching at fleas. Parasites are nasty, and you'll want to eliminate any that have infested your Corgi.

External Parasites

Depending on where you live and the time of year you get your puppy, you may already have encountered fleas or ticks.

Fleas

Fleas are nasty little critters, and if your dog happens to be allergic to flea saliva, they can make your pet miserable. Your first indication that your dog may have fleas is if he is scratching and/or biting himself. Have your dog roll over, and check his stomach, especially toward the groin, where the hair is thinner. You may see fleas scurrying for cover, or you may just see black flecks. Scrape off a few of these flecks and place on a dampened paper towel. If the specks turn red, those flecks are "flea dirt," and that red is your dog's blood. Pushing the fur the wrong way on your dog's back and head may

Intact males may be susceptible to prostatic hypertrophy, which is a benign enlargement of the prostate. Neutering prevents prostate problems and may curb aggression and end marking in the house.

Besides the benefits of no unwanted litters, spaying a female before her third heat lowers the chance of mammary tumors. After the third heat, there is not much difference in the incidence of these tumors, but spaying does end the chance of pyometra and other reproductive also uncover fleas. If you do discover fleas, be aggressive in flea control.

Many different products are on the market, including very effective topical treatments, and your veterinarian can help you choose the one best suited for your dog. If your dog is heavily infested with fleas, a bath using a flea-fighting shampoo is a good idea to begin with.

Daily vacuuming is as effective as any spray in keeping the flea population down in the house. You can cut up a flea collar and put it in the vacuum bag to help kill the fleas. Also, change the vacuum bag frequently, or you'll be supporting a flea colony in the bag. Wash your dog's bed frequently too, as that is where most of the flea eggs will accumulate. Combing your dog with a flea comb will also help trap the unwanted guests.

Ticks

Ticks may or may not be a problem in your area. If you take long walks in tall

Check your dog for fleas and ticks after he's been playing outside.

grass or through brush, you are more likely to pick up a tick or two than in a backyard. Deer ticks, which are very small, can spread Lyme disease.

Remove ticks gently, using tweezers, or put alcohol on them. Never use a cigarette or anything else that will burn. Undoubtedly, that would get the tick's attention, but you are also apt to burn your dog. If you don't think that you can get the tick off properly or just don't want to try, have your vet do it for you. The important thing is to check your dog on a routine basis if ticks are a problem in your area and not leave them on your dog.

Internal Parasites

Whipworms, hookworms and roundworms can all be discovered by a fecal check.

Heartworms require a blood test, and tapeworm segments are usually evident in the stool and can be seen with the naked eye. Internal parasites can be harder to detect than those living on the

surface, and that's why a fecal check once or twice a year is so important.

Heartworms

Heartworm is a deadly parasite that does not show up in fecal checks but requires a blood test to detect. This parasite can kill or incapacitate your dog, and the cure can be almost as bad as the disease. It is much better to prevent it than cure it. The medicine needed to kill the heartworms is quite harsh, and the dog must be restricted from activity for four to six weeks. In severe cases, the dog will need to be crated for three to four weeks. Once the worms are dead, there's a danger of clumps of dead worms causing clots before they disintegrate. Activity on the dog's part increases this risk. Heartworm larvae develop in mosquitoes and are passed to the dog when a mosquito bites him. These larvae move to the chambers of the right side of the dog's heart. There, the worms mature and produce microfilariae, which circulate in the blood until another mosquito ingests them after feeding on the dog. Adult heartworms can completely fill the heart chambers. An infected dog may tire easily and develop a cough. An annual blood test can tell whether any microfilariae are present. Talk to your veterinarian about a monthly heartworm preventive for your dog. Some prevent only heartworms; some also include chemicals that kill other

Ask the Expert

HOW TO KEEP YOUR CORGI HEALTHY

—Lucy Jones, veterinarian and breeder

Q: Overall, Corgis are a healthy breed, but as a veterinarian, what recommendations do you make to keep them that way?

A: Diet and weight control are at the top of my list. That, and they need outdoor time and people time. Don't just put your Corgi out in the yard and forget him. Take him places. Take walks, or let him ride along in the car. Corgis love to go places with their people.

worms, such as hookworms. A shot that is effective for up to six months is also available.

Hookworms

Hookworm eggs are passed in the feces and can live in the soil. They may also be passed from a bitch to her puppies. Hookworms feed on the blood of their host and can cause fatal anemia in puppies. A fecal sample can determine if your dog has hookworms, and a medicine to kill the worms will be dispensed. Interceptor, which is also a heartworm preventive, will kill hookworms, but other products are available as well. Talk to your veterinarian about the right one for your dog.

Roundworms

Roundworms contaminate the soil, and the eggs are able to remain in the soil for years. Most puppies are born with these worms because the larvae are able to live in an intermediate host, in this case the bitch, but not infect her. This is why it is necessary to deworm young puppies. Breeders generally worm puppies automatically, or they may take a fecal sample to their veterinarian to determine if the puppies have roundworms. Puppies with roundworms may have diarrhea and/or vomit, or they will have distended abdomens all the time. They may be thin, as the worms are getting most of the nourishment. If you suspect that your puppy has roundworms, take a fecal sample to your vet, and if the test is positive, proper medication will be prescribed.

Tapeworms

Tapeworms are the least harmful of the worms that may infest your dog and the most common. Your dog can acquire tapeworms from swallowing a flea, so

As a breed, Corgis are generally healthy dogs.

controlling the flea population is one of the best ways to prevent tapeworms in your dog. Tapeworm segments are visible in the stool and will look like small grains of rice. Check your dog's stool periodically for evidence of tapeworms. If you find tapeworm segments, contact your veterinarian for treatment, which generally requires just one dose.

Whipworms

Whipworms can cause deep inflammation of the colon. If your dog has periodic bouts of diarrhea with mucus and blood evident, he may have whipworms. Again, contaminated soil is to blame. Once whipworms are in your soil, paving the entire area is about the only way to totally solve the problem. Protect your dog from worms with periodic fecal checks, and use the medicine your vet prescribes to get rid of them.

Breed-Specific Illnesses

Corgis, as a breed, are generally healthy, but some health issues do appear from time to time. However, with regular checkups, vaccinations as required, and a balanced diet, your Corgi should stay healthy for many years.

Disk Problems

Some veterinarians feel that disk problems are common in Corgis, but others don't think that they are any more susceptible than any other breed. Corgis may be more at risk because of the combination of short legs and enthusiasm. Jumping off of high places can cause a disk injury. If you're playing flying disc with your Corgi, keep the disc low so that he is not leaping and twisting. Also, watch your dog's weight. Corgis love to eat, and it's easy for them to gain weight, which can also lead to back problems.

Invertebral Disk Disease

Although Corgis don't have the long backs of a Dachshund, their short legs and their fearlessness at leaping and jumping can lead to intervertebral disk disease. When the spongy disks between the spinal vertebrae become injured, they ooze up and can put pressure on the spinal cord. You may notice that your dog can't go up and down stairs or that his hind legs may be slipping out from under him, especially on smooth surfaces. Touching him on the back may hurt. In mild cases, weeks of crate rest and no stair climbing may be enough to let the disks heal. In severe cases, a dog may lose feeling in his legs and feet, and surgery may be required. Don't let your Corgi leap on and off of furniture or make large jumps to catch a toy. That can help prevent injuries to the disks.

Degenerative Myelopathy

Degenerative myelopathy is a progressive disease of the spinal cord that eventually leads to complete paralysis of the hind legs. The good news is that it's not painful; the bad news is that there's no cure. In the beginning, your dog may seem wobbly in the hindquarters and may have trouble staying upright on slick surfaces. Stairs may become a problem. The dog may drag one foot or the other. A DNA test is now offered by the Orthopedic Foundation for Animals (OFA) that can determine if a dog is carrying the gene for this disease.

Glaucoma

Glaucoma is an increase in fluid in the eye, resulting

in increased pressure and eventual blindness. It is a painful condition, and your dog may be irritable, have decreased appetite, and may not want to play. The dog may squint or rub his eye. Symptoms may include cloudy eyes, dilated pupils, tearing, or bloodshot eyes. Caught early, drops and oral medication can help slow the progress of the disease, but eventually, your dog will need surgery, which may save some of the vision in the eye.

Hip Dysplasia

Hip dysplasia is a genetic disease, so the best way to avoid it is to get a puppy whose parents have been judged clear by the OFA. In hip dysplasia, the ball of the hip joint doesn't fit properly into the socket, causing abnormal wear. Eventually, arthritis forms, and it becomes more and more painful for the dog to move naturally. A dysplastic dog may limp or be stiff, especially after exercise. It may be hard for the dog to manage stairs. The dog may "bunny hop," moving the hind legs together, rather than moving each leg separately. X-rays can determine if your dog has hip dysplasia. The condition can be corrected with surgery,

including replacing the joint, but this is expensive. Many dogs can lead full lives with prescribed medication.

Progressive Retinal Atrophy

Progressive retinal atrophy (PRA) seems to be familial in Corgis. If a dog has PRA, he will go blind in both eyes simultaneously. The loss of sight is gradual and is not painful. There is no treatment, but with a few precautions, most blind dogs can lead happy lives. The first thing you might notice is that your dog's eyes are dilated, and they seem to have more shine or glow. At this point, the dog is probably already suffering from night blindness. There is a genetic marker for PRA in Cardigan Welsh Corgis, but this marker has not yet been found in Pembrokes.

Von Willebrand's Disease

Von Willebrand's is an inherited blood disorder that inhibits the blood's ability to clot. Corgis with von Willebrand's may have nose bleeds and bleed from the gums. If they are injured, the wound will bleed longer than normal. Surgery that requires transfusions can be an issue. The disease can be managed, but there is no cure and no specific treatment. Make sure that your breeder tested your dog's parents for this disease, and ask for the results.

General Illnesses

The following illnesses and diseases are no more prevalent in Corgis than in any other breed of dog, but they are common problems that you may see in your dog.

Allergies

Corgis are not prone to skin problems, but any dog can develop an allergy. Dogs can be allergic to foods, molds, or pollens, just like people. Usually, these allergies cause itchy skin. If the discomfort is seasonal, it's probably "something in the air."

Food Allergy

If it's continuous, it could be the food you're feeding him. If your dog's reaction is not too severe, you may have the time to try different foods, such as foods with rice as the basic grain instead of corn. If there's a severe reaction, once again, you'll need a trip to the vet. She may want to run some tests or may suggest a food made of all one product. These special diets have just one ingredient, such as duck; then, by gradually adding other foods, you can eventually determine the exact cause of the allergy. It's a lengthy process and fortunately, most dogs don't need to go this route.

HOW TO GIVE MEDICINE

If your veterinarian prescribes medicine for your Corgi, it will usually be in pill form. Most Corgis are chowhounds, so your Corgi may gulp down a pill as is or even if it's just lying on top of his food. Otherwise, a bit of food around the pill will make it acceptable. You can use a spoonful of yogurt, a dab of peanut butter, some cream cheese, a bite of hot dog, some canned dog food, or almost anything that your dog will eat quickly, taking the pill with it.

Liquids are a bit harder. Pull your dog's lower lip out on the side, making a little pocket into which you can pour the liquid. Then quickly close the dog's mouth and gently stroke his throat until he swallows. Having a helper hold your dog might be a good idea.

With eye drops or ointment, hold your Corgi between your legs and approach the eye from behind. Gently hold open the eye a bit and squeeze in the drops or ointment. With ointments, close the eye tightly so that the salve will melt and won't just stick to his eyelashes.

Have your vet check your dog's teeth at least once a year.

Hot Spots

If your dog is allergic to flea saliva, he will bite and scratch where a flea has bitten, and he may do damage to himself if the irritation drives him to continuous biting and scratching at one spot. Whether or not he is allergic, if he is licking or biting at an area for whatever reason, that area can develop into a hot spot. Hot spots are raw, red, oozy-looking spots that can spread and get infected if not treated. I use a triple antibiotic salve on hot spots, and this seems to clear them up. If a hot spot doesn't get better or continues to get larger, check with your veterinarian.

Mange

Mange is another skin problem to watch for. There are two types of mange, both caused by tiny mites. With sarcoptic mange, there is intense itching, and with advanced cases, skin lesions and hair loss. It is treated with ivermectin, and externally with sulfur dips. Revolution, a monthly flea and tick preventative, is another effective treatment. Treatment usually lasts for three weeks. The dog's bedding should be thoroughly disinfected or thrown away.

Demodectic mange is passed from the mother dog to her puppies and affects puppies between the ages of three and ten months. You may notice hair loss around the eyes, lips, or on the forelegs or the tips of the ears. Demodectic mange is usually diagnosed from skin scrapings. A special shampoo may be recommended, and ivermectin will again be used.

Demodectic mange, if not widespread on the dog's body, may go away on its own. If it spreads beyond small, localized areas, the dog may need up to a year of treatment.

Cancer

As in humans, cancer in dogs can take many different forms, showing different symptoms and responding to different treatments. Cancer can be in the form of a tumor, so see your veterinarian if you

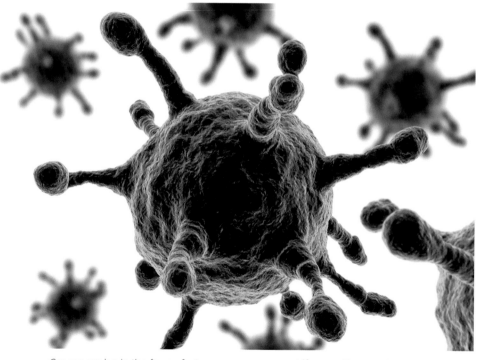

Cancer can be in the form of a tumor, so see your vet if you notice any strange lumps or bumps on your dog.

notice any strange lumps or bumps on your Corgi. Caught early, many cancers can be removed with surgery. Lymphoma, or cancer of the lymph system, may first be detected through swollen glands on either side of your dog's face, much like mumps in people. Chemotherapy can help extend your dog's life, and dogs typically don't have as bad a reaction to chemo as people do. Some cancers respond to radiation.

Possibly the first indication of cancer of an internal organ may be that your dog is no longer interested in food, or there may be a change in his feces. Whenever you notice something not normal about your dog, see your veterinarian. Advances continue in the treatment of canine cancer, and many forms can be cured.

Dental Disease

Dental care is easily overlooked, but statistics show that 75 percent of all dogs have some kind of periodontal problem by the time they are four years old, so include your Corgi's mouth and teeth in every health check. Although dogs are not as susceptible to tooth decay as humans, they do develop plaque, which if not removed, hardens to tartar. Tartar, in turn, can cause abscesses, and the bacteria from those abscesses can circulate in the system and lead to pneumonia or heart, liver, or kidney problems.

There may come a time when your veterinarian recommends a professional cleaning for your dog's teeth. Not all dogs are alike, of course. Some dogs may need their teeth cleaned every six months; some may go their entire lives without needing a professional cleaning. Have your veterinarian check your dog's teeth at least once a year, and if you notice that your Corgi's breath smells more than his normal "dog breath," or if he is drooling or pawing at his mouth, or is having trouble eating hard food and no longer wants to chew on toys or bones, make an appointment with your veterinarian.

Alternative Therapies

Alternative therapies are gaining in popularity, and many veterinarians are either learning more about these therapies themselves or are happy to refer their patients to qualified practitioners.

Acupuncture

Acupuncture involves using hair-fine needles to stimulate acupoints and help with healing. Acupoints are areas on the skin that contain concentrated levels of nerve endings, lymphatics, and blood vessels. Acupuncture is frequently used for treating chronic conditions like arthritis and allergies, and to relieve pain and inflammation. Epilepsy may also be helped by acupuncture. Acupuncture can also help speed healing. Increased blood flow from the acupuncture treatment aids healing, and less pain medicine is needed when acupuncture is used.

To learn more about acupuncture or to find a veterinarian in your area who practices acupuncture, the International Veterinary Acupuncture Society (IVAS) lists certified veterinary acupuncturists by state at its website www.ivas.org.

Chiropractic

Chiropractic treatment is the manipulation of the spine and connected bones, on the theory that when the spine and these bones are even slightly displaced, nerves become irritated. Chiropractors gently push the bones back into their correct place. If your dog is very active—for instance, if you are doing agility with him—the occasional chiropractic adjustment may be just what he needs. Even a couch potato may benefit from an adjustment if he lands wrong jumping down from his comfy nest.

Many people take their dogs to chiropractors for humans if they can't find a veterinarian who offers the service. If that's your choice, make sure your veterinarian has examined your dog first to ensure that there's no other cause, like a tumor, that might be pushing on his spine.

Herbal Remedies

The acupuncture website mentioned earlier (www.ivas.org) can also guide

When correctly used, herbal medicines may be gentler and safer than synthetic compounds.

you to veterinarians who use herbal remedies. A doctor may have TCM listed after her name, indicating that she practices traditional Chinese medicine, including the use of herbs in treatment. When correctly used, herbal medicines may be gentler and safer than synthetic compounds.

Bach flower essences are often mentioned along with herbal and homeopathic treatments. In the 1800s, English doctor Edward Bach began

Physically, senior dogs can still do just about anything they are used to doing.

Homeopathy

Homeopathy is the theory that like heals like. A substance is diluted in several stages so that it is safe and free from side effects yet is still powerful enough to act as a healing agent. Homeopathic remedies come in tablets, powders, granules, liquids, and ointments. This idea may be hard to understand, but a homeopathic practitioner compared it to vaccines, where the "like" substance may be weakened or killed germs that are used to prevent the disease they would cause if they were full strength.

Senior Dogs

Dogs tend to be classified as "senior" when they are seven years old, but outside of the possibility of a graying muzzle, you probably won't notice any changes in your Corgi. Most Corgis just keep being active. Your Corgi might not have quite as much bounce or want to play fetch for quite as long a time, but physically, Corgis can still do just about anything they are used to doing.

Just because your Corgi is still active doesn't mean that there aren't changes going on within. His metabolism may change. A food he has always liked may now disagree with him. He may need his teeth cleaned more often. Continue your annual veterinary checkups, and don't ignore strange lumps or bumps that may appear.

studying the healing properties of various plants. He eventually identified 38 flowers and trees with specific healing properties for emotional and behavioral problems, such as shyness, fear, and anxiety. Rescue Remedy is a mixture of five of the single essences and is effective in cases of shock, collapse, and trauma. Many holistic veterinarians recommend Rescue Remedy as a part of a dog's first-aid kit. Check your local health food store for this product.

Check It Out

HEALTH CHECKLIST

To stay healthy, your dog will need:
- ✓ basic first-aid supplies
- ✓ dog toothbrush and toothpaste
- ✓ fresh water always available
- ✓ house and yard clear of poisonous products
- ✓ regular veterinary checkups
- ✓ top-quality food
- ✓ vaccinations as necessary

As your Corgi ages, he may become hard of hearing or start to lose his eyesight. It may be hard to tell if your Corgi is losing his hearing or just being selective, but if he doesn't even look your way when you call him, he may not hear you. Fortunately, dogs do understand sign language, and you can still communicate with your Corgi with hand signals.

Blind dogs can still enjoy life, but you will need to make adjustments. First, don't rearrange the furniture. Block off stairways until you have worked with your dog and know that he can go up and down safely. Use different textures of flooring to let him know where he is.

Place a nonslip mat at the bottom and top of flights of stairs. Use a runner through a room that may have lots of obstacles. You can also use different scents, such as a small dab of perfume at the top and bottom of stairs, for instance, or a bit of vanilla at doorways. Supervise outdoor time, and if you are taking a walk, remember to be your Corgi's eyes so that he doesn't run into a tree or stumble off the curb.

A senior dog may require a bit more work, but he is also a steady, calmer pal, and remembering all the good times you've had over the years will make the extra effort worth it.

Resources

Associations and Organizations

Breed Clubs

American Kennel Club (AKC)
5580 Centerview Drive
Raleigh, NC 27606
Telephone: (919) 233-9767
Fax: (919) 233-3627
E-Mail: info@akc.org
www.akc.org

Canadian Kennel Club (CKC)
89 Skyway Avenue, Suite 100
Etobicoke, Ontario M9W 6R4
Telephone: (416) 675-5511
Fax: (416) 675-6506
E-Mail: information@ckc.ca
www.ckc.ca

Federation Cynologique Internationale (FCI)
Secretariat General de la FCI
Place Albert 1er, 13
B – 6530 Thuin
Belgique
www.fci.be

Pembroke Welsh Corgi Association (Canada)
www.pembrokewelshcorgis.ca

Pembroke Welsh Corgi Club of America, Inc. (PWCCA)
www.pembrokecorgi.org

The Kennel Club
1 Clarges Street
London
W1J 8AB
Telephone: 0870 606 6750
Fax: 0207 518 1058
www.the-kennel-club.org.uk

The Welsh Corgi Club (England)
www.the-welsh-corgi-club.co.uk

United Kennel Club (UKC)
100 E. Kilgore Road
Kalamazoo, MI 49002-5584
Telephone: (269) 343-9020
Fax: (269) 343-7037
E-Mail: pbickell@ukcdogs.com
www.ukcdogs.com

Pet Sitters

National Association of Professional Pet Sitters
15000 Commerce Parkway, Suite C
Mt. Laurel, New Jersey 08054
Telephone: (856) 439-0324
Fax: (856) 439-0525
E-Mail: napps@ahint.com
www.petsitters.org

Pet Sitters International
201 East King Street
King, NC 27021-9161
Telephone: (336) 983-9222
Fax: (336) 983-5266
E-Mail: info@petsit.com
www.petsit.com

Rescue Organizations and Animal Welfare Groups

American Humane Association (AHA)
63 Inverness Drive East
Englewood, CO 80112
Telephone: (303) 792-9900
Fax: 792-5333
www.americanhumane.org

American Society for the Prevention of Cruelty to Animals (ASPCA)
424 E. 92nd Street
New York, NY 10128-6804
Telephone: (212) 876-7700
www.aspca.org

The Humane Society of the United States
(HSUS)
2100 L Street, NW
Washington DC 20037
Telephone: (202) 452-1100
www.hsus.org

Royal Society for the Prevention of Cruelty to
Animals (RSPCA)
RSPCA Enquiries Service
Wilberforce Way, Southwater,
Horsham, West Sussex RH13 9RS
United Kingdom
Telephone: 0870 3335 999
Fax: 0870 7530 284
www.rspca.org.uk

Sports

International Agility Link (IAL)
Global Administrator: Steve Drinkwater
E-Mail: yunde@powerup.au
www.agilityclick.com/~ial

The World Canine Freestyle Organization, Inc.
P.O. Box 350122
Brooklyn, NY 11235
Telephone: (718) 332-8336
Fax: (718) 646-2686
E-Mail: WCFODOGS@aol.com
www.worldcaninefreestyle.org

Therapy

Delta Society
875 124th Ave, NE, Suite 101
Bellevue, WA 98005
Telephone: (425) 679-5500
Fax: (425) 679-5539
E-Mail: info@DeltaSociety.org
www.deltasociety.org

Therapy Dogs Inc.
P.O. Box 20227
Cheyenne WY 82003
Telephone: (877) 843-7364
Fax: (307) 638-2079
E-Mail: therapydogsinc@qwestoffice.net
www.therapydogs.com

Therapy Dogs International (TDI)
88 Bartley Road
Flanders, NJ 07836
Telephone: (973) 252-9800
Fax: (973) 252-7171
E-Mail: tdi@gti.net
www.tdi-dog.org

Training

Association of Pet Dog Trainers (APDT)
150 Executive Center Drive Box 35
Greenville, SC 29615
Telephone: (800) PET-DOGS
Fax: (864) 331-0767
E-Mail: information@apdt.com
www.apdt.com

International Association of Animal Behavior
Consultants (IAABC)
565 Callery Road
Cranberry Township, PA 16066
E-Mail: info@iaabc.org
www.iaabc.org

National Association of Dog Obedience Instructors (NADOI)
PMB 369
729 Grapevine Hwy.
Hurst, TX 76054-2085
www.nadoi.org

Veterinary and Health Resources

Academy of Veterinary Homeopathy (AVH)
P.O. Box 9280
Wilmington, DE 19809
Telephone: (866) 652-1590
Fax: (866) 652-1590
www.theavh.org

American Academy of Veterinary Acupuncture (AAVA)
P.O. Box 1058
Glastonbury, CT 06033
Telephone: (860) 632-9911
Fax: (860) 659-8772
www.aava.org

American Animal Hospital Association (AAHA)
12575 W. Bayaud Ave.
Lakewood, CO 80228
Telephone: (303) 986-2800
Fax: (303) 986-1700
E-Mail: info@aahanet.org
www.aahanet.org/index.cfm

American College of Veterinary Internal Medicine (ACVIM)
1997 Wadsworth Blvd., Suite A
Lakewood, CO 80214-5293
Telephone: (800) 245-9081
Fax: (303) 231-0880
Email: ACVIM@ACVIM.org
www.acvim.org

American College of Veterinary Ophthalmologists (ACVO)

P.O. Box 1311
Meridian, ID 83860
Telephone: (208) 466-7624
Fax: (208) 466-7693
E-Mail: office09@acvo.com
www.acvo.com

American Holistic Veterinary Medical Association (AHVMA)
2218 Old Emmorton Road
Bel Air, MD 21015
Telephone: (410) 569-0795
Fax: (410) 569-2346
E-Mail: office@ahvma.org
www.ahvma.org

American Veterinary Medical Association (AVMA)
1931 North Meacham Road, Suite 100
Schaumburg, IL 60173-4360
Telephone: (847) 925-8070
Fax: (847) 925-1329
E-Mail: avmainfo@avma.org
www.avma.org

ASPCA Animal Poison Control Center
Telephone: (888) 426-4435
www.aspca.org

British Veterinary Association (BVA)
7 Mansfield Street
London
W1G 9NQ
Telephone: 0207 636 6541
Fax: 0207 908 6349
E-Mail: bvahq@bva.co.uk
www.bva.co.uk

Canine Eye Registration Foundation (CERF)
VMDB/CERF
1717 Philo Rd
P O Box 3007
Urbana, IL 61803-3007
Telephone: (217) 693-4800
Fax: (217) 693-4801
E-Mail: CERF@vmbd.org
www.vmdb.org

Orthopedic Foundation for Animals (OFA)
2300 NE Nifong Blvd
Columbus, Missouri 65201-3856
Telephone: (573) 442-0418
Fax: (573) 875-5073
Email: ofa@offa.org
www.offa.org

US Food and Drug Administration Center for Veterinary Medicine (CVM)
7519 Standish Place
HFV-12
Rockville, MD 20855-0001
Telephone: (240) 276-9300 or (888) INFO-FDA
http://www.fda.gov/cvm

Publications
Books
Anderson, Teoti. *The Super Simple Guide to Housetraining.* Neptune City: TFH: Publications, 2004.

Anne, Jonna, with Mary Straus. *The Healthy Dog Cookbook: 50 Nutritious and Delicious Recipes Your Dog Will Love.* UK: Ivy Press Limited, 2008.

Dainty, Suellen. *50 Games to Play With Your Dog.* UK: Ivy Press Limited, 2007.

Morgan, Diane. *Good Dogkeeping.* Neptune City: TFH Publications, 2005.

Magazines
AKC Family Dog
American Kennel Club
260 Madison Avenue
New York, NY 10016
Telephone: (800) 490-5675
E-Mail: familydog@akc.org
www.akc.org/pubs/familydog

AKC Gazette
American Kennel Club
260 Madison Avenue
New York, NY 10016
Telephone: (800) 533-7323
E-Mail: gazette@akc.org
www.akc.org/pubs/gazette

Dog & Kennel
Pet Publishing, Inc.
7-L Dundas Circle
Greensboro, NC 27407
Telephone: (336) 292-4272
Fax: (336) 292-4272
E-Mail: info@petpublishing.com
www.dogandkennel.com

Dogs Monthly
Ascot House
High Street, Ascot,
Berkshire SL5 7JG
United Kingdom
Telephone: 0870 730 8433
Fax: 0870 730 8431
E-Mail: admin@rtc-associates.freeserve.co.uk
www.corsini.co.uk/dogsmonthly

Websites
Nylabone
www.nylabone.com

TFH Publications, Inc.
www.tfh.com

Index

Note: Boldfaced numbers indicate illustrations.

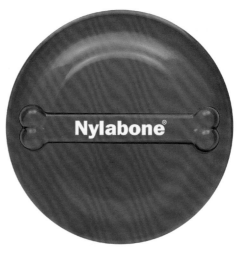

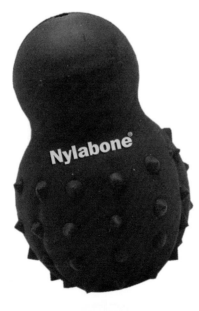

Photo Credits

B&T Media Group Inc. (Shutterstock): front cover, spine

Jonathan Brizendine (Shutterstock): 86

Andrew Chin (Shutterstock): 42

dmvphotos (Shutterstock): 50

BW Folsom (Shutterstock): 49

EE_Gritsun (Shutterstock): 39

Jostein Hauge (Shutterstock): 117

Mark Herreid (Shutterstock): 98

Sebastian Kaulitzki (Shutterstock): 127

Laila Kazakevica (Shutterstock): 118

Naturablichter (Shutterstock): 9

Iurii Osadchi (Shutterstock): 30

RCPPHOTO (Shutterstock): 52

Gastev Roman (Shutterstock): 8

rebvt (Shutterstock): 129

Annette Shaff (Shutterstock): 36

steamroller_blues (Shutterstock): 18

Leah Anne Thompson (Shutterstock): 112

Tootles (Shutterstock): 37

H. Tuller (Shutterstock): 33 (bottom)

Luna Vandoome (Shutterstock): 109

Yan Wen (Shutterstock): 26, 73

Andrey Yurlov (Shutterstock): 106

All other photos courtesy of Isabelle Francais and TFH archives

Dedication

For Marsha, always, and for Kathy Smith, who bred Griffin and Rhiannon.

Acknowledgments

Huge thanks to my experts, Julia Clough, Pam Dennison, and Dr. Lucy Jones.

About the Author

Susan M. Ewing has been "in dogs" since 1977. She owned and operated a boarding kennel and enjoys showing and participating in various performance events. She is affiliated with the Dog Writers Association of America (DWAA) and is president of the Cat Writers Association (CWA). Since 1964, Susan has been writing professionally for newspapers, magazines, and radio. She writes a weekly column, "The Pet Pen," for *The Post-Journal* (Jamestown, NY). She currently lives in Jamestown, New York, with her husband, Jim, and her Corgis, Rhiannon and Rory.

Nylabone®

JOIN NOW
Club Nylabone
www.nylabone.com
Coupons!
Articles!
Exciting
Features!

He **Plays** Hard.
He **Chews** Hard.

He's a Nylabone® Dog!
Your #1 choice for healthy chews & treats.

Nylabone proudly offers high-quality durable chews,
delicious edible treats, and fun, interactive toys for dogs of all sizes, shapes, and life stages.

Nylabone Products • P.O. Box 427, Neptune, NJ 07754-0427 • 1-800-631-2188 • Fax: 732-988-5466
www.nylabone.com • info@nylabone.com • For more information contact your sales representative or contact us at sales@tfh.com

A318